John Smith

The life of St. Columba

The apostle and patron saint of the ancient Scots and Picts and joint patron of the

Irish

John Smith

The life of St. Columba

The apostle and patron saint of the ancient Scots and Picts and joint patron of the Irish

ISBN/EAN: 9783741166334

Manufactured in Europe, USA, Canada, Australia, Japa

Cover: Foto ©Thomas Meinert / pixelio.de

Manufactured and distributed by brebook publishing software (www.brebook.com)

John Smith

The life of St. Columba

THE
LIFE

OF

St. COLUMBA,

THE APOSTLE AND PATRON SAINT OF THE ANCIENT SCOTS AND PICTS,

AND

JOINT PATRON OF THE IRISH;

Commonly called

COLUM-KILLE, the Apostle of the HIGHLANDS.

BY JOHN SMITH, D. D.

ONE OF THE MINISTERS OF CAMPBELTON;
HONORARY MEMBER OF THE ANTIQUARIAN AND HIGHLAND SOCIETIES
OF SCOTLAND

S. COLUMBA, cognomento *Kille*, Abbas Hienſis, Scotorum et Pictorum Apoſtolus, et utriuſque Scotiæ Patronus; *Appen. Vit. St. Pat.*—— Hiberniæ, Albaniæ, et Inſularum Hebridum Patronus; *Colgan.*—— Seminator religionis in univerſa fere Hibernia et Albania; *Quat. Magiſtri.*——Nulli poſt Apoſtolos—ſecundus; *Notker.*

EDINBURGH:

PRINTED FOR MUNDELL & SON, AND J. MUNDELL, COLLEGE, GLASGOW;
SOLD IN LONDON BY JOHN WRIGHT, PICCADILLY.

1798.

TO

HIS GRACE

THE DUKE OF ARGYLL, PRESIDENT,

AND

TO THE OTHER MEMBERS

OF THE

HIGHLAND SOCIETY OF SCOTLAND,

THE FOLLOWING ACCOUNT

OF THE

LIFE OF ST. COLUMBA,

IS MOST RESPECTFULLY INSCRIBED

BY

THE AUTHOR.

PREFACE.

THERE is implanted in the mind of man a principle of curiosity, which makes him defirous of knowing the manners and cuftoms of others in diftant places and in former times. This defire is particularly ftrong in regard to what relates to one's own country. We then feel a more than ordinary intereft in viewing thofe cuftoms, manners, and modes of thinking and acting, which prevailed in the days of our forefathers.

To fatisfy this curiofity, no mean is fo likely as the particular hiftory, anecdotes, and memoirs of the men who, in their time, made the greateft figure in their country. In this view, the following account of St. COLUMBA may not, perhaps, be unworthy of the perufal of fuch as wifh to know fomething of the ftate of religion and fociety in the Highlands about twelve hundred years ago.

No man ever lived to whom the Highlands and Ifles of Scotland were more indebted than fo St. Columba; and, perhaps, few lived to whom the Britifh ifles in general were under ftronger obligations. It was Columba who kindled that torch which, in the darkeft ages, fhed its kindly rays far beyond the limits of the Highlands, and which contributed much to enlighten even the fouth of Britain : for, according to the teftimony of the venerable Bede, England was indebted, for many of its moft learned and pious divines, to the feminary of learning eftablifhed by Columba, in a remote and obfcure corner of the Highlands. Such are the revolutions effected by Time in this world of ftrange viciffitudes!

In a period in which biography is fo much in vogue, an account of the life of fo extraordinary a man, and of fuch a benefactor to his country and to mankind, may claim fome little attention from thofe who may perhaps at this day be, in part, indebted for their comforts to the fruits of his labour and inftructions. The conqueror of kingdoms may claim our admiration; but the enlightener and civilizer of nations deferves our love, efteem and refpect. The memory of the one, without any imputation of ingratitude, may be fuffered to perifh; but the memory of the other deferves to be honoured.

The general taste at present is for books of a light, gay, and amusing cast. But why may not even the readers of such books diversify their amusement, and bestow an hour or two on the perusal of the history of a man, who may now be considered as so singular and extraordinary a character, that his life may well pass for novel? If, in the midst of gaiety, this should for a moment dispose them to be serious, where would be the great harm? Or, should it lead them to reflect for a little on the power of religion, with its pleasures and prospects, as exhibited in the life of Columba, what reason can they have to think that they should afterwards repent it, or that the time was not well bestowed? Among the many expedients which they use for passing the time, might they not try, for once, how the reading an account of the life of a saint would pass a little of it?

To the man who is truly pious and religious, the life of Columba cannot fail to be entertaining and useful. It will show him the power of Divine grace upon the soul, and the progress that may be made in holiness by a man entirely devoted to God, and aspiring to as high a degree as possible of glory, honour, and immortality. The contemplation of such a life will attract his regard, and powerfully

engage him, in part at leaft, to follow the
example.

But the life of St. Columba is calculated to
be ftill more ufeful to thofe in holy orders; as
it furnifhes them with a lively example of
fidelity and zeal in the difcharge of their important office, and with a fair copy of every
grace and virtue that fhould adorn the facred
character. To examine how other men in the
fame profeffion have difcharged the duty to
which we are called, what manner of men
they have been, and what manner of works
they have done, may lead us to confider what
we ourfelves are, and how we ought to act, fo
as to obtain the WELL-DONE of our LORD,
when we fhall be called to give an account
of our ftewardfhip *.

A laudable fpirit for propagating the gofpel
in foreign parts is at prefent gone abroad. To

---

* The following pages were chiefly drawn up at firft with
this view, and intended to accompany fome difcourfes or
Lectures on the Nature and End of the Sacred Office, but which
the Bookfeller chofe to feparate; that fuch as wifhed only
for the one might have it without the other. Moft of the
Notes, and the Appendix, were, in confequence of this, drawn
up partly for the fake of other readers, and may be paffed over
by fuch as do not choofe to be interrupted by fuch matters
as they contain.

the miffionaries employed in this important work, it may be ufeful to have the example of a man who devoted his life to the fame bufinefs; to know the means which he ufed, and the manner in which he acted, fo as to have attained [fuch wonderful fuccefs. For few, if any, fince the days of the Apoftles had more fuccefs in preaching the gofpel to the heathens, than the venerable St. Columba.—May God, for Chrift's fake, endow all who are engaged in the fame office with a portion of the fame fpirit !

b

CONTENTS.

THE
LIFE
OF
ST. COLUMBA.

THE life of St. Columba [1], the Apoſtle of
the Highlands and Weſtern Iſles of Scotland,
and the founder and firſt abbot of the famous
monaſtery of Iona [2], was written by two of his

[1] The venerable Bede, Cambden, and ſome others, call
him *Columbanus*. In the language of the country, he is called
Colum-cille (or Colum of the Cells), from his having founded
ſo many churches and monaſteries. The addition of *cille*,
ſeems to have been early made to his original name Colum.
" Sanctus COLUMBA abbas, quem Angli vocant Colum-
" killum, doctrina et virtutibus mirabilis, in illo glorioſo cœ-
" nobio quod in inſula Yi conſtruxerat degens," &c. *Vit.
Kentigern.* Another eminent Iriſh ſaint, of the name of
Columbanus, who flouriſhed about the ſame period, is often
confounded with St. Columba.

[2] Its ancient name was *I*, *Hi*, or *Aoi* (as written in the

fucceffors, Cummin and Adomnan [3]. The former of thefe wrote about fixty, and the latter about eighty-three years after the death of the faint; fo that they had very good opportunities of coming at the knowledge of every part of his life and character.

But, unhappily, it feems not to have been the

Annals of Ulfter), which were Latinized into Hyona, or Iona. The common name of it now is I-colum-kill (the Ifle of Colum of the Cells), included in one of the parifhes of the Ifland of Mull. Its venerable ruins ftill command refpect; and the popular belief, founded upon a prophetic diftich a-fcribed to St. Columba, is, that they may yet recover their ancient fplendour.

An I mo chridhe, I mo ghraidh
 An aite guth manaich bidh geum bà;
Ach mun tig an faoghal gu crich
 Bithidh I mar a bha.

O facred dome, and my belov'd abode!
Whofe walls now echo to the praife of God;
The time fhall come when lauding monks fhall ceafe,
And lowing herds here occupy their place
But better ages fhall thereafter come,
And praife re-echo in this facred dome.

The firft part of the prophecy was literally fulfilled for ages, till the prefent noble proprietor (the Duke of Argyll) caufed the facred ground to be enclofed with a fufficient wall. Before then, the cathedral was ufed fometimes as a penn for cattle. *Sic tranfit gloria mundi!*

[3] Both wrote in excellent Latin, fuch as perhaps no other compofition of thofe times can rival.

object of thofe good men to delineate the real
life and character of the faint, but to give a
marvellous detail of vifions, prophecies, and miracles, which they boldly afcribe to him. It is
but candid to fuppofe that they themfelves believed what they wrote, and that their writings
may have been of ufe in thofe ages of credulity and fable; although, in our more enlightened times, they rather difguft than edify in that
antiquated form. It is therefore neceffary, if
we would perufe the life of this great and holy
man with patience and with profit, to ftrip it
of that marvellous garb with which it has been
fo long invefted, to feparate the fact from the
fable, and to fhow the faint in his real character.

In attempting this, I fhall make no further
ufe of that mafs of wonders which I mentioned,
than as it ferves to illuftrate the character of
Columba, or the fpirit of the times in which he
lived. Of thofe marvellous relations I do not
profefs to believe any; nor would I be fo bold
as to deny them all. In circumftances fuch as
thofe in which Columba ftood, called forth to
extirpate an old and inveterate fuperftition,
and to eftablifh the true religion upon its ruins,
to furmount the prejudices of a barbarous people, and to contend with powerful and artful
priefts, we cannot, without prefumption, fay

A ij

how far it might be fit that God fhould countenance the labours of his faithful fervant, and
vouchfafe him even by figns and wonders, as
he often did to his minifters in fuch cafes, a
clear and decided victory. A reflection fomewhat fimilar to this is made by one of his biographers, after mentioning the iffue of a conteft to which the faint was challenged by the
Pictifh priefts or druids [3], before an immenfe
crowd of fpectators near the royal palace at
Lochnefs [4].

But of thefe matters, as we muft allow ourfelves to be very incompetent judges, it is our
wifdom to be filent. The life of Columba is
abundantly uncommon and interefting without
them; and his example, as it will in that cafe
be the more imitable, will be alfo the more
ufeful: and with a view to imitation in ufefulnefs only do I attempt to unfold this holy man's
life and character [5].

---

[3] The druids are faid to have had a college in I, before
the time of St. Columba; and tradition ftill points out their
burying ground, by the name of *Cloadh nan Druidhnach*.

[4] Adomn. l. ii. c. 25. " Deus omnipotens—talibus mira-
" culorum virtutibus, coram plebe gentilica, illuftre fuum ma-
" nifeftavit nomen."

[5] " Nam fi miracula falfiffima concedamus, nequaquam
" fequitur ad hiftoriam, geographiam, morefque pertinentia
" nullius effe fidei; cum Livius plenus fit miraculorum, et mi-
" racula Vefpafiani apud Tacitum notiffima." *Pinkerton*
Pref. ad Vit. SS. Scot.

Columba was a native of Ireland, defcended from the royal family of that kingdom, and nearly allied to the kings of Scotland [6]. Like many others who made a confpicuous figure in the world, his birth is faid to have been preceded by fome extraordinary circumftances. Maveth, the difciple of St. Patrick, is faid to have predicted the birth and name of Columba, and the lafting glory which he fhould acquire by converting the Weftern Ifles to Chriftianity [7].

His mother alfo, when with child of the faint, dreamed one night that a perfon, whofe figure and mien feemed to denote him to be more than human, had prefented her with a veil or garment of the moft beautiful texture and colours; that in a little time, however, he refum-

[6] His father was Felim the fon of Fergus, who was grandfon of the great Nial, king of Ireland; and the mother of Felim was Aithne, daughter of Lorn, who firft reigned, in conjunction with his brother Fergus, over the Scots or Dalreudini in Argyllfhire. In thofe times noblemen were not feldom the preachers of the gofpel; and it is probable they may be fo again, when they fhall find that neither their perfons nor their property can be fecure without it.

[7] Adomn. Præf.—ficuti nobis ab antiquis traditum expertis compertum habetur. " In noviffimis (inquit) temporibus fæ-" culi, filius nafciturus eft, cujus nomen COLUMBA, per om-" nes infularum oceani provincias divulgabitur notum : novif-" fimaque orbis tempora clare illuftrabit."

ed his gift, and raiſing and expanding it in the
ſky, allowed it to fly through heaven. As it
flew, it continued to extend itſelf on all hands,
over mountains and plains, till at length it covered an expanſe which her eye was not able
to meaſure. Finding what ſhe had once poſſeſſed thus gone out of her reach, and likely to
be irrecoverably loſt, ſhe could not help ex-
preſſing her ſorrow and regret, till the angel
thus addreſſed her : " Be not grieved at not
" being allowed to retain this valuable gift but
" for a very ſhort time. It is an emblem of
" that child of which thou art ſoon to be the
" mother : for him hath God ordained, as one
" of his prophets, to be extenſively uſeful upon
" earth, and to lead an innumerable company
" of ſouls to heaven ⁸."

  Columba was born in the year 521, and his
parents being thus, as they believed, admoniſh-
ed of the part which their ſon was deſtined to
act in life, and to which they ſoon perceived
his genius and early diſpoſition to piety to be
peculiarly adapted, loſt no time in providing
him with ſuch education as tended to qualify
him for the ſacred office. They firſt put him
under the care of Cruinechan, a devout preſ-
byter, who diſcovered, as he thought, in his

⁸ Cum. 1. Ad. iii. 1. Angelus Domini in ſomnis, &c.

difciple while yet a child, extraordinary fymptoms of his future glory and greatnefs ⁹.

Some time after he ftudied under Finnian
Bifhop of Clonard, a man (according to Ware ¹)
of confiderable learning, who was fo much
charmed with the piety of Columba, that
though he was yet but a youth, he ufed to give
him the appellation of SAINT; and believed,
from his uniformly holy and regular life, that
he had obtained from God an angel from heaven to be his companion and guardian ².

Fenbar, alfo a bifhop and faint, is mentioned as one of Columba's mafters ³; and likewife
Gemman, a teacher of Leinfter, who, like his
other mafters, ufed to give his pupil the name
of SAINT; and notwithftanding the great dif-
parity of their years, feems to have treated him
rather as a companion and friend, than as a
fcholar; fometimes afking his opinion about
the moft dark and myfterious difpenfations of
Providence. Under him the piety of Colum-

---

⁹ Ad. iii. 2. Spiritus fancti gratiam fuper fuum intellexit al-
lumnum cœlitus effufam.—Globum quippe igneum fuper
pueruli dormientis faciem vidit.

¹ Script. Hibern. p. 10. He died in 552.

² Cum. 4. Ad. iii. 4. En—Sanctum Columbam qui fui
commeatus meruit habere focium angelum cœlicolam.

³ Ad. ii. 1. Apud S. Fendbarum—Sapientiam facræ fcripturæ addifcens.

ba, now in deacon's orders, became fo diftinguifhed, that his fame was already fpread over
a great part of the kingdom, to which the following incident feems to have contributed not
a little. One day as the old man read his book
in the fields, a young girl, purfued by a barba-
rian, fled to him for protection. He immediately cried to his pupil, who was reading at a
little diftance. The aid of both was unavail-
ing ; the ruffian, with one thruft of his fpear,
left her dead at their feet. " Ah!" faid Gemman, " how long will God, the righteous Judge,
" allow this atrocious deed to go unpunifhed ?"
" The foul of the murderer," replied Columba,
" may yet be in hell as foon as that of the mur-
" dered in heaven." At that inftant they obferved the unhappy man fall dead at fome diftance, a facrifice, it is probable, to the violence
of his own paffions, though afcribed by the
people to the appeal which was made to heaven by Gemman and Columba [4].

Our faint fpent alfo fome time under St. Ciaran [5], the father and founder of the monaftery
of Clon, upon the Shenan. For this man, fo

[4] Ad. ii. 26.
[5] He preached to the Attacotti or Dalreudini of Kintyre,
and died in 594. *Ware.* From him the parifh of Kil-chiaran,
of late called Campbelton, takes its name. (*Stat. Acc. of Campbelton*). Several traditions concerning him are ftill preferved

Venerable for his piety and zeal in preaching the gofpel, Columba retained always the ftrongeft affection, and wrote a facred ode upon his death, in which he celebrates his virtues [6].

---

in the parifh. One of them is, that he had an old horfe which ufed to beg for him, and bring to his cave whatever the charity of the well difpofed in the neighbourhood had put in his panniers. One day a wicked fellow put out the poor horfe's eyes, in confequence of which he loft his way, fell over a rock, and perifhed. Next day the culprit was ftung by a ferpent, and his life defpaired of; upon which the faint being called, prayed for him, and applied unguents, by which his life was faved; but with the lofs of his eye-fight. Such traditions, in favour of religion and morals, are more than harmlefs. The eftimation in which this faint was held in his lifetime may be judged of from the vifion of St. Baithen, who dreamed that he had feen three fplendid chairs prepared in heaven, one of gold, one of filver, and one of glafs; and all agreed in the interpretation of their being intended for Ciaran, Laifran and Columba. *Colgan. Vit. S. Molaffii.*

[6] The beginning of this ode or hymn, with fome other hymns, preferved by Colgan (*in Traide Thaumaturga*) may be feen in the appendix.

There is alfo extant a beautiful Irifh ode of his, being a *Farewell* to his monaftery in Ireland, when he fet out for Scotland. The imagery of this piece is fingular. Seven angels, Uriel, Ithiel, &c. are reprefented as having the charge of this monaftery, each his own day in fucceffion throughout the week, and then returning to give the recording angel an account of what paffed in the monaftery; an idea well calculated to excite in the monks the ftricteft attention to conduct, and the ftrongeft defire to excel.

B

How much Columba was loved and revered
by his companions, during his ftay in this
place, appears from the wonderful veneration
with which he was received when he came to
vifit them fome time afterwards [7]. All the
people in the monaftery and its neighbourhood
poured out to meet him, kiffed him with the
utmoft reverence and affection, and finging
hymns and pfalms of praife, led him to their
church, furrounded with a rail of wood, carried by four men, to prevent his being incom-
moded by fo immenfe a multitude [8].

Whether he remained in the monaftery of
Clon till the death of Ciaran is not mentioned;
but in the fucceeding year, the 28th of his
age, we are told that he founded the monaftery of Darmagh or Durrough [9], where a copy
of the four Evangelifts, which he had tranfcribed, was extant, according to Ware, in the
laft century, when this author wrote his hiftory.

---

[7] Circa, 550.

[8] Ad. i. 3. Univerfi undique—hymnifque et laudibus re-
fonantes, honorifice ad ecclefiam perducebant : quandamque
de lignis pyramidem erga fanctum deambulantem conftringen-
tes, a quatuor viris æque ambulantibus fupportari fecerunt :
ne videlicet fanctus fenior Columba ejufdem fratrum multi-
tudinis conftipatione moleftaretur.

[9] Ad. i. 3. cum not. Pinkert. et Bede, iii. 4. (now Derry.)

It was probably in the interval, betwixt founding this monaftery and coming to Britain, that Columba vifited feveral foreign countries, in which his piety, learning, and other accomplifhments, procured him the higheft regard and efteem. From fome of the eaftern churches he is faid to have borrowed the model of his monaftic rule[1]; in Italy he is faid to have founded a monaftery; and in France he was folicited by King Sigibert, who made him large promifes, to remain with him. But Columba, whofe ambition was to be ufeful rather than great, told him, that he was fo far from coveting the wealth of others, that for Chrift's fake, he had already renounced his own[2].

How much time Columba fpent in travelling, or when he returned home, we cannot fay. Indeed, the chronological notices in the memoirs of his life which are left to us, are fo few as to preclude every attempt at a regular feries of his hiftory. We have, however, abundant materials for developing his life and cha-

---

[1] Sir R. Twifden, on the Rife of Monaftic States.

[2] Columbanus ipfe (ut Abbas Walafridus fcribit), a Sigiberto Francorum rege magnifice pollicitatione ne regno fuo decederet invitatus, refpondet, " Non decere videlicet ut alienas divitias amplecterentur qui nomine Chrifti fuas dereliquiffent." Camden in Hibern.

racter; and this is what we have already profeffed to be our object.

Ireland had now for a long time enjoyed the
light of the Gofpel, and abounded in faints and
learned men, while the ifles and northern parts
of Scotland were ftill covered with darknefs,
and in the fhackles of fuperftition. On thofe
difmal regions, therefore, Columba looked with
a pitying eye, and, however forbidding the
profpect, refolved to become the Apoftle of the
Highlands. Accordingly, in the year 563 [3],
he fet out in a wicker boat covered with hides [4],
accompanied by twelve of his friends [5] and fol-

---

[3] Vid. Cum. 22. et not. Pink. Bede fays two years later.
[4] " Anno 565, venit de Hibernia prefbyter et abhas, habitu et
" vita monachi infignis, nomine Columbanus, Britanniam;
" prædicaturus verbum Dei provinciis feptentrionalium Pic-
" torum, hoc eft, eis qui arduis atque horrentibus montium
" jugis, ab auftralibus eorum funt regionibus fequeftrati."
iii. 4.
[4] Called in Gaelic *curach;* the place where he landed in
Icolumkill is ftill called *Port-a-churaich.*
[5] Hence probably the monks of Iona got the name of
" the Apoftolic Order," to which none were better entitled.
                                        Epitome Biblioth. Gefneri.
" This was the origin of the order of the *Culdees* in Scot-
" land; an order of which Columba was the founder. He and
" his followers were diftinguifhed for learning, purity of faith,
" and fanctity of life. Bede, in what he meant as a cenfure,
" commends them highly, when he fays, ' They preached on-
' ly fuch works of charity and piety as they could learn

lowers, and landed in the Isle of Hi or Iona, near the confines of the Scottish and Pictish territories [5]. This place he probably chose, as being conveniently situated for his attending to the important concerns which he had to manage in Ireland, as well as for carrying on the work which he had in view in Scotland. Besides, if he should succeed in procuring a grant of it, he might discover in it those pro-perties which were generally sought for in the site of religious houses [6].

Columba was now in the 42d year of his

---

[f] from the prophetical, evangelical, and apostolical writings.'
" They firmly opposed the errors and superstitions of the
" church of Rome, till towards the end of the 12th century,
" when they were at length overpowered and supplanted by a
" new race of monks, as inferior to them in learning and
" piety, as they surpassed them in wealth and ceremonies."
See *Ledwich's Antiq. of Ireland.*

[5] " Insula *Pictorum* quædam monstratur in oris,
" Fluctivago suspensa salo, cognomine *Hii,*
" Qua sanctus Domini requiescit carne Columba."
Vit. Blaimhac.

Bede says, that Iona belonged then to the Picts. The Irish Annals, and after them Usher, say it belonged to the Scots; and Adomnan, who knew best, seems in effect to say the same, when he tells us that their territories were separated by the *Dorsum Britanniæ* (or Drim-albin) ; " inter quos utros-
" que dorsi Britanici montes distermini." Ad. ii. 46.

[6] Perambulavit igitur (Kentigernus) terram, explorans si-tus locorum, qualitates aëris, glebæ ubertatem, pratorum et

age, and needed all his vigour of mind and body in encountering thofe difficulties which
prefented themfelves when he undertook the
converfion of the northern Picts to Chriftianity. The nation was in fo barbarous'a ftate,
that fome of them, regardlefs of the fanctity'of
his character, made more than once an attempt' upon his life [7] ; and the king, not more
civilized than his people, ordered his gate to
be fhut when the holy man 'firft approached
it [8]. The priefts or druids, too, as they were
moft interefted, fo they were moft forward to
oppofe' him [9], and wanted neither eloquence,

---

pafcuarum ac filvarum fufficientiam, et cætera quæ expectant
ad edificandi monafterii commoditatem. *Vit. Kentig.*

[7] Ad. i. 35. Trans dorfum Britanniæ (Drim-albin), &c.
Here an enemy, in the dead of night, fet fire to the village
in which he flept. At another time, in the Ifle of Himba, a
ruffian, called *Lamb-der*, rufhed upon him with his fpear,
which, one of his difciples, *Finduchan*, haftily ftepping in to
fave his mafter, received in his own bofom, and was faved
only by the thicknefs of his *cuculla*, or leathern jacket, from
being transfixed. Id. ii. 25. The *cuchul craicinn* is mentioned
in old poems. In the rude ftate of all focieties, men were
partly dreffed in fkins; but fo are they in its moft polifhed
ftate alfo.

[8] Id. ii. 36. Rex (Brudeus) faftu elatus regio, munitionis
fuæ non aperiret portas. Brude reigned from A. D. 557 to
587.

[9] Magi (Hibern. Druidh) in quantum poterant prohibere
conabantur. Id. i. 38. et ii. 33, 35.

influence, or art, to effect their purpofe. The country itfelf was wild, woody, and mountainous, and greatly infefted with wild beafts, from which the life of the faint feems to have been more than once in imminent danger [9]. And, what appears to have been the greateft difficulty of all, he was fo little mafter of the dialect of that people, at leaft of fome among them, or for the firft while, as to need an interpreter when he preached to them the words of falvation [1].

Befides all this, the aufterity of his own manners, fometimes fafting for whole days, and watching and praying for whole nights [2]; fubmitting to conftant fatigue of body and anxiety of mind abroad, or the moft intenfe application to ftudy at home [3]; and withal fo felf-

---

[9] Id. ii. 27, 28.

[1] Id. ii. 33. Some antiquaries think, that the language of the Picts and Irifh Scots, at this period, differed only in dialect, and that this only inftance, in which mention is made of an interpreter, may, refer to fome ftranger of another nation. Indeed Columba, in his general intercourfe with the Picts, feems to converfe with them, in their common language, with eafe; and the names of the perfons and places mentioned are generally Irifh or Gaelic. This fubject admits of difcuffion.

[2] Id. iii. 18.

[3] Nullum etiam unius horæ intervallum tranfire poterat, quo non orationi, aut lectioni, vel fcriptioni, vel etiam alicui operationi incumberet. Id. i. 1.

denied and crucified to the world, as to reject what we are now accuſtomed to conſider as its innocent comforts and enjoyments [4];—theſe were, all of them, circumſtances very unfavourable in appearance to his making many proſelytes : And we may add, that the ſtrictneſs of his *monaſtic rule* [5], which impoſed heavy ſpiritual taſks, enforced by the ſanction of bodily chaſtiſements, would alſo ſeem an unſurmountable bar to his gaining many diſeiples to his cloiſters.

Notwithſtanding all this, however, the labours of Columba were attended with a very aſtoniſhing degree of ſucceſs. In the courſe of a few years, the greater part of the Pictiſh kingdom was converted to the Chriſtian faith ; monaſteries were erected in many places, and churches every where eſtabliſhed. Columba, as Primate [6], ſuperintended and directed all

---

[4] At the age of 76, Columba's bed was the bare ground, and a ſtone his pillow. Id. iii. 23.

[5] Holſtein. Cod. Regul. " Dura et laborioſa monaſteri- " ola imperia," are his own words in ſpeaking of it. Ad. ii. 40.

[6] *Notker* ſays, he was " Primate of *all* the Iriſh churches ;" which he was made at the council of *Drimceat*. Forbes (*on Tithes*) obſerves, that he and his ſucceſſors extended their juriſdiction not only over all the ecclefiaſtics of the Highlands and Iſles, but alſo over the monaſteries of Dunkeld, Abernethy, Kilvi-

the affairs of the Pictish, and much of the
Scottish and Irish churches, and was highly
reverenced, not only by the king of the
Picts [7], but also by all the neighbouring
princes [8], who courted his acquaintance, and
liberally affisted him in his expenfive under-
takings [9]. Wherever he visited abroad, he
was received with the highest demonstration
both of respect and joy ; crowds attended him

---

mont (or St. Andrew's), Abercorn; Monimusk, Kirkcaldy,
&c, Bede (iii. 4.) and many others have remarked as fingular, that Columba and his succesfors, though only abbots,
should exercife a jurifdiction over bishops.　But though Columba was not ambitious of high titles, he had the best right
to the fuperiority of all the churches and monasteries which
he himfelf had founded ; and thefe were very many, both in
Scotland and Ireland.　Magnus Odonellus (*Vita Colum.*) fays
that above 300 churches had been establifhed by Columba.
Jocelin (*Vit. S. Pat.*) calls him " the founder of 100 mona-
" fteries ;" and the Irifh Annals (4 *Magift. ann.* 592.) fay,
that, next to St. Patrick, he was the chief inftrument of
establifhing the gofpel in almoft all Ireland : " Columba, a-
" poftolus Albaniæ, id eft Scotiæ Albienfis, præcipuus poft
" S. Patricium præco veritatis, et feminator religionis in uni-
" verfa fere Hibernia."

[7] Sanctum et venerabilem virum regnator (Brudeus), fuæ
omnibus vitæ reliquis diebus, valde magna honoravit honorifi-
centia.　Ad. ii. 36.

[8] Ad. iii. 5. et i. 14, 15.

[9] Eftates in different parts of the kingdom, as in Galway,
&c. were annexed to his monaftery.　Vid. *Pennant's Tour.*

C

on the road; and to the place where he lodged
at night, the neighbourhood sent stores of pro-
vifions to entertain him [1]: And when the
multiplicity of his bufinefs allowed him to ftay
at home, he was reforted to for aid and advice,
as a phyfician both of foul and body, by multitudes of every rank and denomination [2].
Even the place of his refidence was confidered
as peculiarly holy; and to fleep in the duft of
it became, for ages, an object of ambition to
kings and princes [3]. His monaftery was the
chief feminary of learning at the time, perhaps,
in Europe, and the nurfery from which not
only all the monafteries, and above 300

---

[1] Vit. Kentig. c. 39. Ad. i. 3. et i. 51. Conallus epif-
copus Culcrathin collectis a populo pene innumerabilibus
xeniis, beato viro hofpitium præparavit, turba fequente multa,
&c.

[2] Rex (Brudeus) mifit, &c. Ad. ii. 34. Rex Rodercus
de Petra Cluoith, mifit, &c. Id. i. 15.

[3] According to Buchannan, 48 kings of Scotland (too
many), four of Ireland, and eight of Norway, were buried
in Iona.

In Adomnan frequent mention is made of Aidan (or Aodhan MacGhabbrain), who reigned over the Scots in what is
now called Argyllfhire; of Brude, who reigned over the
Picts at Invernefs; and of Roderic, who reigned over the
Strath-clyde Britons, and lived at Petra Cluoith, or Dun-
Briton, now corrupted into Dumbarton, except by the Highlanders, who ftill call it by the old name.

churches, which he himfelf had eftablifhed, but alfo many of thofe in neighbouring nations, were fupplied with learned divines and able paftors [4].

How then are we to account for this great and rapid fuccefs of Columba; for there is no certainty of his having been endowed either with the gift of prophecy, or with the power of working miracles? No doubt the Providence of God fmiled upon his labours; and perhaps we might difcover a coincidence of favourable circumftances in the hiftory of the times. But we are more concerned to feek for the caufe in the character and conduct of the man; by which he was rendered fo eminently qualified for the facred office, and fo fuccefsful, under God, in the difcharge of it. The inveftigation of this fubject is deferving of the attention of minifters, and not unworthy of the curiofity of men.

That Columba's talents were of a very fuperior kind, is not to be doubted [5]. An uncommon greatnefs of foul is marked in every

---

[4] " Qui infulam *Hii* incolebant monachi Scoticæ nationis, " fcientiam divinæ cognitionis, libenter ac fine invidia, po- " pulo Anglorum communicare curabant." *Bedæ Hift.* v. 23. See more on this fubject in the Appendix.

[5] ——ingenio optimus. *Ad.* i. 1.

part of his extenſive ſchemes ; and the happy execution and ſuccefs of them are pregnant proofs of wifdom, perſeverance, zeal, and abi-. lities.

Firmneſs and fortitude are no léfs conſpicu-ous in Columba's charaċter. When he came to Britain, he ſeems to have been well aware of the difficulty of his undertaking, and of the time and toil which it ſhould coſt him to ac-compliſh it. But inſtead of ſhrinking back, he only prayed to God to give him thirty years of life [7], which he devoted to his ſervice, hoping that by the aid of Divine grace, he ſhould in that period accompliſh his deſigns.

We muſt alſo allow Columba a very extra-ordinary ſhare of addreſs, perſonal accompliſh-ments, and colloquial talents, when he could ſo effeċtually recommend himſelf wherever he went, though a perfeċt ſtranger, as to be ſoon reſpeċted, loved and cheriſhed ; and when he could gain ſuch aſcendency over ſo many princes, as to be revered and patronized by all of them, when all of them were in a ſtate of barbariſm, and ſeldom at peace among them-ſelves ;—a ſure proof this, that his conduċt was always guarded with the utmoſt caution and prudence ; that he never ſtepped out of his

[7] Cum. 16. et Ad. iii. 22.

own line, nor took any concern whatever in
ftate affairs, when he could by any means a-
void it. Once, indeed, he put the crown on
the head of the Scottifh king Aidan ; but he
feems to have done it with reluctance, and
pleads the ftrong neceffity of having been com-
pelled to it by a fupernatural agent [8].

The fame prudence and addrefs may be difcovered in his having been able to maintain
good difcipline, order and fubordination in fo
many monafteries, and fo remote from one another ;—to direct the religious affairs of a great
part of feveral nations, differing confiderably
in language and cuftoms ;—to fuperintend the
education of youth, and furnifh fo many
churches with fit paftors ;—and to do all this
in fuch a manner that the growing love and
veneration of men feem to have invariably
kept pace with his years. To which we may
add, that his fagacity in difcovering probable
effects from known caufes, may have probably
acquired him the reputation of being a pro-
phet.

---

[8] Angelus fanctum [dum recufaret] percuffit flagello, cujus
livofum in ejus latere veftigium omnibus fuæ diebus permanfit
vitæ ; hocque intulit verbum, " Si nolueris, &c. percutiam te
" iterato : et fic per tres noctes, &c." Ad. iii. 5. et Cum. 5.
This powerful argument could not be refifted.

To thefe talents, which were accompanied
with the moft engaging addrefs, and a pleafant
cheerful countenance, was joined another very
effential property in a preacher, a moft powerful and commanding voice, which Adomnan
fays he could on occafions raife fo as to re-
femble peals of thunder [8], and make it to be
diftinctly heard at a mile's diftance, when he
chanted pfalms.

That thefe natural endowments of Columba
were highly cultivated by the beft education
and learning which the times could afford, is
clear from the mention already made of fo many of his mafters. A particular account or his
ftudies, indeed, is not tranfmitted to us; but
they feem by no means to have been confined
to that profeffion which he followed, but to
have extended much further into the general
circle of fcience. For his knowledge of phyfic, or fkill in healing difeafes, was fo great
that his cures were often confidered as miracles [9]. And in the hiftory, laws, and cuftoms

---

[8] Ad. i. 38. " Vox ejus—inftar alicujus formidabilis toni-
" trui elevata eft." " Qui ultra mille paffuum longinqui-
" tatem ftabant, fic clare eandem audiebant vocem, ut illos
" quos canebat verficulos, etiam per fingulas poffent diftin-
" guere fyllabas."

[9] Ad. ii. 4, 5, 7, 6, 34, &c. In fome of Columba's cures,
fuppofed by Adomnan to be miraculous, mention is made of

of different nations, he was fo well verfed, that he made a principal figure in the great council held at DRIMCEAT, about the right of fucceffion to the Scottifh throne [1].

But whatever degree of knowledge and education Columba might have received in his earlier years, he never ceafed, by intenfe ftudy and application, to add to it. Every moment which fo active and pious a life could fpare from its main bufinefs, was devoted to ftudy [2].

---

his fprinkling the difeafed perfon or beaft with water, in which a cake or medicament had been infufed, and of his making ufe of water into which he had put fome ftone or foffil. From this probably fprung fome fuperftitious practices, not yet quite extinct in the Highlands, where many families have fome pebble or cryftal (called *leug*), and fprinkle difeafed cattle with the water in which it has been immerfed. Columba's medicine is loft, and only the form of adminiftering it is retained.

[1] Magna concio Drimacet, in qua fuit ColumkilI, &c. *Annal. Ulton.* ad ann. 574. *O'Conner's Differt. et O'Flagherty's Ogygia.* The conteft was between *Aodh Mac-Amireich* king of Ireland, and *Aidan* king of the Scots. This Aidan (or *Aodhan MacGhabhrain*), who was then king of the Scots (*Dalreudini*), had his refidence in Kintyre, and was the moft famed of all the old Scottifh kings for his warlike exploits. We find him fometimes conquering in Ireland, and fometimes carrying his arms to the other hand, as far as Northumberland.

[2] Ad. i. 1. " Vel fcriptioni vel lectioni," &c. Id. iii. 18. In Himba per tres dies totidemque noctes, neque manducans

Sometimes he heard his difciples read, and fometimes he read himfelf; fometimes he tranfcribed, and fometimes read what had been tranfcribed by others[3]. In his life, we find mention made occafionally of various books of his writing and copying[4]; and as he wifhed his ufefulnefs to man to be commenfurate with the moments of his life, and to make a part of the ultimate preparation for heaven, he fpent fome time in tranfcribing the Pfalter, on that very night on which he knew and told he was to be tranflated to eternal day[5].

---

neque bibens—fcripturarum facrarum obfcura quæque et difficillima—difcere, &c.

[3] Id. i. 35. et i. 23. " In hoc tuo pfalterio, nec una fu-" perflua reperietur litera, nec alia deeffe; excepta *I* vocali, " quæ fola deeft."

It was by thus teaching the ufe of letters, and eftablifhing a feminary of learning, that Columba did the greateft fervice to his country. He thus kindled a light which fhone in a dark place for many generations, and by its kindly beams cherifhed the feed which he had fowed, and brought it forward to an abundant harveft. Without this, all his perfonal virtues and perfonal labours could have produced but a comparatively fmall and temporary effect.

[4] Ad. ii. 8, 45, &c.—folium S. Columbæ, &c.—libris ftilo ipfius defcriptis, &c. no lefs than 300, fays Odonellus.

[5] Ad. ii. 23. et Cum. 20. They are only the ignorant or ungrateful who give monks the epithet of *lazy*. To them we

In the character of Columba, talents, learning, and a conftant application to ftudy, make a very confpicuous figure ; but a ftill more ftriking part of it, is an early, uniform, and ftrong fpirit of piety. Devoted from his birth to the fervice of God, and ardently bent on the purfuit of holinefs, he feems to have almoft reached the goal before others think of ftarting in the race. The appellation of *faint* was given him, as we have already feen, while he was yet a child. But far from refting in any meafure of fanctity acquired in early life, he inceffantly laboured after higher and higher degrees of it to his lateft day. In every moment, in every motion, and in every action of his life, he feems to have maintained upon his fpirit a lively fenfe, a ftrong impreffion, and al-

owe the prefervation of almoft all that has reached us of the learning, arts and fciences of the ancients. To them we owe many ufeful inventions, and efpecially the firft leffons in agriculture, the moft important of all arts to mankind. In the rude and predatory age of Columba, with what pleafure muft we read of his monks at their daily labour in the field, of heaps of grain in his granary, of prefents of it fent to his neighbours to fow their land, and of his having a Saxon baker in his monaftery, when there was not another, we may believe, in the whole kingdom ? We are ftill more agreeably furprifed to find monafteries in thofe times furnifhed with orchards, as appears from the mention made of their apple trees. *Ad.* iii. 10. et ii. 2. &c.

D

moſt a clear viſion of the preſence of God. And ſurely a ſaint, without being accounted a viſionary, may be allowed to ſee with the eyes of the mind, and by the light of divine truth, the preſence of ſpiritual eſſences, with as clear and ſatisfying a conviction of their reality, as that which he has of outward objects, in open day. Such ſeems to have been the caſe with Columba[1]; and therefore we need not wonder, if, in every thing, ſmall and great, he had ſo conſtant a regard to God. " When do you " purpoſe to ſail, Columba?" ſaid the Magician or Druid[2], Broichan. " On the third day " hence," replied the ſaint, " if it be the will " of God, and that I am then alive." " You " cannot," ſays Broichan; " for I will raiſe " contrary winds, and ſpread over you miſts " and darkneſs." " All things," anſwered the ſaint, " are under the controul of the Omnipo- " tent God; and every motion of mine is un- " dertaken in his name, and entirely guided " by his direction[3]."

In every affair of leſſer moment, Columba

---

[1] Gratia Sancti Spiritus ſuper eum abunde effuſa—arcana manifeſtata videbat—et luce clarius aperta mundiſſimi cordis oculis patebant. Ad. ii. 18. et Cum. xiii.

[2] Druidb is ſtill the Gaelic name for a magician. The per- ſon named here was probably the chief Pictiſh prieſt.

[3] Ad. ii. 35.

shows the same regard to God, and the same
spirit of piety. If he only ascended his little
car, when a car became necessary, he implored
upon it the benediction of Him who only could
give it power to carry, and whose providence
could keep it from falling [4]. If the milk from
the fold passed him every day, every day it
had his solemn benediction [5]. If he looked on
the corn by which his family was to be fed,
he could not fail of saying, Blessed be God!
or God bless it [6]! If the wind blew this way
or that, he took occasion from it, either to pray
to God, or to thank him; with an eye to such
of his friends as the course of it concerned [7].
If he visited a pious friend, the first salutations
were mixed with alleluiahs, and the soul had
its spiritual entertainment before the body was
yet refreshed.

[4] Id. ii. 44. Currum ab eo prius benedictum ascendit.

[5] Id. ii. 15. Juvenis portans vasculum novo plenum lacte,
dicit ad Sanctum, ut juxta morem tale benediceret onus.

[6] Id. iii. 23. Horreum, quod intrans Sanctus cum bene-
dixisset, et duos in eo frugum sequestratos acervos, hoc intulit verbum cum gratiarum actione, inquiens, &c.

[7] Id. ii. 43. Nostris commembribus in periculo constitutis
mente compati debemus fratribus, et Dominum exorare cum
eis, ut Austrum flantem ventum, in Aquilonem convertat;
qui videlicet Aquiloneus ventus navem Cormaci de periculis
retrahat. Et post gaudenter grates Deo agit,—quia Austrum
in Aquilonarem convertit flatum, &c.

" Saint Columba, or Columkil," fays the author of the Life of Kentigern, " left his ifland
" of *Yi*, to fee the faint of Glafgow. When
" he approached the monaftery, all went forth
" with facred fongs to meet him; while he
" and his party alfo came forward, finging
" their melodious alleluiahs. And after thefe
" godly men had met, abundance of fpiritual
" entertainment preceded their bodily refresh-
" ment [8]."

Perhaps fome, who judge only by the manners of modern times, may fuppofe fome oftentation is here mixed with piety. But the manners even of faints, taking a tincture from the
times, are very different now from what they
were then; and piety, even where it may be
genuine and true, is much lefs fervent. In
thofe primitive and pious times, if two good

---

[8] Omnefque (ex parte Kentigerni) canebant, *In viis Domini quam magna eft gloria Domini!* Et iterum fubjunxerunt,
Via juftorum recta facta eft, et iter fanctorum præparatum eft.
Ex parte Sancti Columbæ, dulcifona modulabant voce, *Ibunt
fancti de virtute in virtutem; videbitur Deus deorum in Syon cum
alleluia.*—Convenientes—divinorum eloquiorum prius fpiritua-
libus epulis faginati, poftmodum corporeo alimento fefe refi-
ciunt.—Alter alterius baculum, in pignus quoddam et tefti-
monium mutuæ dilectionis in Chrifto fufcepit.—After having
thus exchanged ftaves, in token of mutual regard, the two
faints fpent a few days together " in converfing on divine
fubjects, and on matters relative to the falvation of fouls."
Vit. Kentigerni, c. 39. et 40.

men walked together on the road, they could
solace themselves under the fatigues of their
journey by singing the Psalms of David, and
refresh themselves when they sat down by reading a portion of the scriptures [9]. If they did
so now, they would be rated as wrong-headed
enthusiasts, or charged with ostentation, and
perhaps hypocrisy. Columba's piety, however,
was so far from being ostentatious, that its lu-
stre was nowhere so conspicuous as in retire-
ment and solitude. Hence the strong desire of
some of his disciples to find an opportunity of
being sometimes the secret witnesses of the ear-
nestness, or rather ecstasy of their master's private devotion. And from the accounts which
they give us of what they saw and heard, we
cannot greatly blame their curiosity [1].

These accounts, it is true, have somewhat of
a miraculous air, in the relation of Cumin and
Adomnan ; and perhaps they ought to be re-

---

[9] Ninianum (cum Plebia fratre) suo more laborem itineris
hymnis solari Davidicis ;—et cum repausarent,—sacra lectione
recreabant animos. _Vit. Ninian._ c. 9. _Vid. etiam Jerom. ad
Nepot._

[1] Frater-explorator (sanctum) expansis manibus ad coelum
orantem, oculosque ad coelum elevantem conspiceret ;—et
sancti angeli advolantes induti albis vestibus, &c. Ad. iii. 16.
21, &c. Alio in tempore dum intra obseratam domum in
Himba—carmina quaedam spiritualia, et ante inaudita decan-
tari ab eo audiebantur. _Id._ iii. 18.

ceived with some grains of allowance. Yet it
is not for us to say, whether a man of such ex-
alted piety, and of so heavenly a frame of
mind, under labours which needed uncommon
support and consolation, might not, on some
special occasions, have enjoyed a higher degree of communion with God, and stronger
manifestations of his favour, than fall within
the experience, or perhaps belief of ordinary
Christians. In these accounts, we find frequent mention of a heavenly light seen at
times to shine around him, while engaged in
devotion [*]. This is so foreign to our experience, that we might find it easier to doubt or
deny the truth of the fact, than to give a sa-
tisfying account of it. But in things that are
too high for us, modesty becomes us. We

_____

[*] Ad. i. 1. Cœlestis ingens claritudinis lumen, et in noctis
tenebris et in luce diei, super eum aliquando, quibusdam ex
fratribus, diversis et separatis vicibus apparuit effusum.

Id. iii. 19. Sicuti nullius æstivum et meridionalem solem
rectis et irreverberatis potest intueri oculis, sic et illam cœle-
stem claritudinem ille *Virgnous*, qui viderat, sustinere nullo
poterat modo.

Id. c. 20. Alia itidem nocte quidam de fratribus, *Colgius*
nomine, totam videt ecclesiam cœlesti luce repleri, &c.

Id. c. 17. Alio in tempore, dum missarum solennia cele-
brarentur, S. *Brendanus* quemdam crinosum igneum globum,
et valde luminosum, de vertice S. Columbæ ascendentem
vidit.

know that fuch appearances were familiar to other holy men, when thofe angels who were their miniftering fpirits did, for wife and gracious purpofes, manifeft their prefence. Thus, when the angel who inftructed Daniel manifefted himfelf, it was as the appearance of lightning; when the angel appeared to Peter, a light fhone in the prifon ; and when our Saviour, after his afcenfion, manifefted his prefence to Saul in the way to Damafcus, and to John in Patmos, a heavenly glory fhone around with fo much brightnefs, that mortal eyes could not endure its fplendour. It is not for us to limit the Holy One of Ifrael, and fay when, or when not, fuch manifeftations were neceffary or proper. It is not for us to fay, whether God might not favour fuch a man as Columba, and in fuch circumftances, with fome extraordinary manifeftations of his prefence, and with fome fenfible manifeftations of the prefence and fociety of celeftial beings [3]. Be this as it may, he himfelf, as well as his difciples, was under the influence of fuch a belief, as appears from his having been heard (when not aware

---

[3] Ad. iii. 16. Adomnan fays, that one of Columba's private praying places was, from thefe manifeftations, called in his time *Gnoc-aingeal* (the Hill of the Angels); which name it ftill retains.

of it) as addreffing his fpeech to attendant fpirits ⁴. And it is certain, that this belief would
greatly contribute to enliven his piety, and
animate his devotion. Nor is it improbable
that it was founded in reality, if we confider
that he was fo far from wifhing to have thefe
matters publifhed, that, under the fanction of
a folemn promife or oath, he commonly charged the few who accidentally came to know
them, that, in his lifetime at leaft, they fhould
never fpeak of them ⁵.

---

⁴ Id. iii. 15. It may be obferved here, that Columba ad-
dreffes angels in a ftyle the very reverfe of prayer or invoca-
tion, confidering them only as fellow-fervants or miniftering
fpirits. " Angelo Domini, qui nunc inter vos ftabat, *juffi*,"
&c. " I bade an angel of the Lord, who juft now ftood
" among us, to fave one of the brethren juft falling from
" the top of a high houfe : and, how amazing is the fpeed
" of angels ! quick as lightning, and in the twinkling of an
" eye, the angel reached him, though at a great diftance,
" before he reached the ground, and faved him from fuffer-
" ing the fmalleft hurt."

A man falling from the top of a very high houfe (" de cul-
" mine enormis fabricæ," *Notker*) and not hurt, was no bad
proof of the miraculous interpofition to which Columba afcribed
his fafety. The attendance of angels is a pleafing confidera-
tion to the pious Chriftian.

⁵ Id. i. 44. Flexis genibus, per nomen excelfi Dei mihi
promittas, hoc te obfcuriffimum facramentum nulli unquam
hominum, cunctis diebus vitæ meæ enarraturum. *Id.* iii. 15.

Of Columba's piety, however, a more un-
equivocal proof was, his having lived, I may
fay, a life of prayer and of praife. To public
prayers, morning and evening, he was fo attentive, that he feems never to have allowed
himfelf to difpenfe with the performance of
them, in any place, or on any pretence whatever. Thus, in the midft of infidels, enemies,
fcoffers and difturbers of his devotion, when
he had no houfe to cover him, we find him
keep up his cuftom of glorifying God by ftated
and public worfhip [6]. When at home, this
fervice was performed by him in the church,
where we find him punctually attending, even
on the laft day of his life [7].

Befides thefe public prayers, the monaftic
rule of Columba enjoined other very confiderable exercifes. It required the monks to " af-
" femble thrice every night, and as often in
" the day. In every office of the day they
" were to ufe prayers, and fing three pfalms.
" In the offices of the night, from October to
" February, they were to fing thirty-fix pfalms
" and twelve anthems at three feveral times :

---

[6] Ad. i. 38. Sanctus, cum paucis fratribus, extra regis
(Brudei) munimentum, dum vefpertinales Dei laudes, ex moro,
celebraret—magi prohibere conabantur—Sanctus 44 m (nunc
45 m) pfalmum decantare cœpit, &c.

[7] Ad. ii. 23.

" through the reft of the year, twenty-one
" pfalms and eight anthems; but on Saturday
" and Sabbath nights, twenty-five pfalms and
" as many anthems [9]." And all this the faint
himfelf performed with fuch alacrity, that he
was the firft to enter the church to midnight
vigils on the very night on which he died [s].

Of Columba's private prayers no particular
account can be expected. But from the frequent mention which is occafionally made of
his praying in his clofet, and in his little ora-
tory, and of his retiring frequently in the day-
time to folitary places, remote from the tumult
and interruption of men; and of his going to
the church, or fome retired place, in the night-
time, while others flept, we fee that his life
and foul was in this holy exercife. So much
fo, indeed, that, though at times his private
prayers were not prolix [t], yet when in places
in which he could attend to prayer and contemplation without being interrupted, we find

---

[s] Holftein. Cod. Regul. *Cit. ap. Walker's Ir. Bards.*

[9] Ad. ii. 23. Media no&e, pulfata perfonante clocca, fef-
tinus furgens ad ecclefiam pergens; citiorque cæteris, &c.

[t] Poft non prolixam orationem (fays *Fergnus*, who had
himfelf prayed privately about an hour in a winter night),
ecclefiam orationis ftudio, aliis quiefcentibus, &c. Columba
ingreditur, &c. *Ad.* iii. 19.

him fometimes continuing in it for whole nights and days, without either eating or drinking [a].

---

[a] Ad. iii. 8, 19, 20, 21, &c. Per tres dies totidemque noctes, intra obferatam et repletam cœlefti claritudine domum manens, nullum ad fe accedere permitteret, neque manducans, neque bibens. De qua videlicet domo immenfæ claritatis radii per rimulas valvarum, et clavium foramina erumpentes noctu vifebantur.

A faft of three days, upon extraordinary and important occafions, was not in thofe times uncommon. The other Columbanus, when he and his companions formed a purpofe of going to convert the *Sclavi*, kept fuch a faft. B. Columbanus juffit triduanum jejunium fieri, et inceffanter mifericordiam Domini implorari, ut eis fuam indicaret voluntatem. *Vit. S. Magni.* Some there were who made fuch fafts their ordinary practice. Adamannus, monafterii in Anglia quod Colodi dicitur, præpofitus, natione Scotus, vir aufteræ converfationis, et fanctæ vitæ, ita ut, præter Dominicam et quintam feriam, nihil in hebdomada penitus comederet, fæpe etiam noctes integras pervigil in oratione tranfigeret. Claruit A. D. 670. *Frithem. de Script. Ecclef.* In aufterity of life, fome of Columba's followers feem to have exceeded their mafter; and fafting (then thought an excellent mean of bringing the body into fubjection to the foul, or of " taming the beaft by " ftinting him in his food"), though now gone out of fafhion, was always one of the marks in their character.

Hic facra Beati membra Cumini folvuntur;
Cujus cœlum penetrans anima cum Angelis gaudet.
Hunc mifit Scotia fines ad Italicos fenem,
Ubi venerandi dogma Columbani fervando,
Vigilans, jejunans, indefeffus, fedulo orans,
Mitis, prudens, pius, fratribus pacificus cunctis.

E ij

It feems alfo to have been his invariable
rule, to undertake no work, nor engage in any
bufinefs, without having firft invoked God [3].
If about to officiate in any minifterial duty, he
would firft implore the Divine Prefence and
aid to enable him to difcharge it properly [4].
If he himfelf, or any of his friends, were to go
any whither, by fea or land, their firft care was
to implore God to be propitious, and their laft
words at parting were folemn prayer and benediction [5]. If he adminiftered medicines for

It is remarkable that moft of thefe faints lived to extreme old
age : this died in his 96th year. *Chron. Bokienf.* Many
lived to 100, St. Patrick to 120.

[3] Dei—in cujus nomine omnes noftri motus, &c. *Ad.* ii. 35.

[4] Id. ii. 9. Infans ad baptizandum offertur iter agenti (in
Ardnamurchan) Sanctus ad proximam declinans rupem, flexis
genibus paulifper oravit ; et poft orationem furgens—aquam
benedixit, *in qua* infantulum baptizavit. From this it appears that baptifm was then performed by immerfion ; as
indeed it was over all the Chriftian church till the beginning
of the 14th century, except in cafes of extreme neceffity, in
which afperfion was allowed. The baptized was immerfed
three times ; in the name of the FATHER, of the SON, and
of the HOLY SPIRIT. The adults were clothed, except their
head and feet, It is a wonder that this fignificant and apoftolic mode was fo eafily laid afide, when fo many frivolous
queftions, about matters of lefs importance, were fo keenly
agitated. *Vid. Bafnage Lect. Antiq.*

[5] Venientes—ut ipfe a Domino poftulans impetraret prof-

the cure of any difeafe, he accompanied them with prayer to the God who healeth [6]. If he adminiftered even counfel or advice, he would accompany it with prayer to him who difpo- feth the heart to liften; and fometimes he would accompany that prayer with fafting. His beft advices, for inftance, could not re- move fome unhappy difference between *Lugne* and his wife in *Rachlin*. He therefore adds, " You two and I muft fpend this day in pray- " er and fafting [7]." This produced the defi- red effect; for the penitent wife at length con- feffed, that fhe found he could obtain from God what to man feemed almoft impoffible.

In feafons of danger and alarm, whether public or private, he always had recourfe to prayer, as the moft effectual way to prevent, or cure, or bear, every evil to which man is fubject. And the better to recommend the fame courfe to others, he ufed to obferve and inftance the return of prayer. Thus, he a- fcribes it to uncommon wreftling in prayer,

---

perum ventum, et—Vade in pace, &c. Id. ii. 14. et i. 18, 19, &c.

[6] Pineam tradit cum benedictione capfellam, invocato Dei nomine, &c. Id. ii. 5. Laborans ophthalmia petram falis, &c. benedictam, &c. ii. 7.

[7] Id. ii. 42.—A much better expedient than the fafhion- able divorce of modern times.

that a raging peſtilence paſſed by his mona.
ſtery ; and to the ſame çauſe (their having
prayed and faſted) he aſcribes its having carried off only one in the monaſtery of that man
of prayer, Baithen [8].

He recommended prayer ſtill further, by re-
preſenting it as extending its efficacy to future
times, and to generations yet unborn ; and
Adomnan gratefully acknowledges, that at
leaſt Columba's own prayers were in his days
productive of ſignal bleſſings. " In our times,"
ſays he, " we are preſerved from another peſti-
" lence, ſo that though it raged through all
" Europe, it hath not viſited our territory ;
" and though we walked, for two years, in the
" midſt of its repeated devaſtations and ruined
" villages in England, the kingdom of our
" good friend Alfred [9], none of us was ever hurt

---

[8] Sanctus in Hyona—remotiorem ab hominibus locum,
aptumque orationi in ſaltibus quæſivit : ibique forti conflictu
dimicabat, &c. Ad. iii. 8.—Jejuniis et orationibus, &ç.

[9] The people of Northumberland were converted to the
Chriſtian faith in the reign of Oſwald, by Aidan and other pious
monks of Iona, in conſequence of which there was much in-
tercourſe between them for a long time after, and many of
the churches and monaſteries throughout England were planted with divines from this ſeminary. We learn from Bede
(v. 16.) that Adomnan, on the occaſion here alluded to,
had been mediating for a peace between Alfred and his countrymen ; that he had preſented Alfred with a copy of his

" by it. Thanks be to God, the efficacy of
" our venerable Father's prayers hath furely
" reached us [1]."

Can any one conceive fuch virtue to be in
prayer, and not be devoted to it? It is certain none could be more fo than Columba;
yet he never neglected the ufe of ordinary
means, in conjunction with prayer. Thus, at

Defcription of the Holy Land, and obtained from him many
prefents. He fays that Adomnan was " vir bonus et fapiens,
" et fcientia fcripturarum nobiliffime inftructus:" to which
Trithemius adds, " Secularium quoque literarum non igna-
" rus, dulcis eloquio, vita et converfatione præclarus."

The converfion of Ofwald's people is faid to have been fa-
cilitated by a vifion recorded by Adomnan. Before a battle
in which Ofwald was to engage with Cathon king of the
Britons (A. D. 635), he dreamed that he had feen a perfon
of angelic form, whofe head feemed to reach the clouds, and
whofe lucid robe covered almoft his whole army. This perfon told him he was Columba, and affured him of the victory; which he accordingly obtained. This relation Adomnan had from his predeceffor, who had heard it from the
mouth of Ofwald; who might naturally enough have fuch a
dream upon fuch an occafion: although it may alfo be faid,
from better authority than Homer, that " dreams at times
" defcend from God."

[1] Ad. ii. 47. In the 6th century about a third of the human fpecies is computed to have been cut off by peftilence.
Gibbon's Hift. In the 7th century, alfo, it raged very much
in Britain. *Bed. Hift.* iii. 27. Annals quoted by Colgan
(An. 684) fay that it raged for three years, and affected

a time when he was in imminent danger at fea, we find him labouring hard in oozing the boat with a bucket [2]; and in the ordinary exercife of his office, we have feen that he was far from thinking that the moft intenfe prayer could fuperfede the neceffity of equal intenfenefs of ftudy.

Of the efficacy of interceffory prayer he had the higheft opinion, and never failed to recommend and practife it. Accordingly, when he had intimation given him that any perfon, however diftant or unconnected, was in danger of any kind, he would immediately retire to the clofet or church, to plead in his behalf [3]; or prayed where he was, if the emergency was too fudden to admit of his going elfewhere [4]. He would alfo, when their cafe prefented it-

---

every fpecies of animals, of which the greater number perifhed.

[2] Ad. ii. 11. The mariners, however, more pious than many of their brethren in our times, infifted on his betaking himfelf to his proper bufinefs, prayer.

[3] Id. ii. 41. Ad ecclefiam currit, flexifque genibus, pro mifellula in Hibernia (in anguftiis parturitionis laborantis) Chriftum de homine natum exorat.

[4] The efficacy of prayer depends, not on the place, but on the heart: yet the heart is apt to be impreffed more in one place than in another. The very fight of a place appropriated to prayer, helps to put the pious heart in a praying frame.

felf to his mind, though engaged in company
or converfation, dart up fudden and fometimes
audible ejaculations in their favour, while his
change of countenance difcovered how much
his heart was concerned [5].

Nor did he fhow his fenfe of the virtue of interceffory prayer only by his own interceffion
for others, but alfo by requefting theirs for
him, and by afcribing fome of his deliverances
more to their prayers than to his own. Being
once, for inftance, overtaken by a tempeft in
the dangerous gulf of *Coire-vrecain*, and in
great danger of being loft, he told thofe who
were with him, that he relied more on the interceffion of his friend St. Kenneth, for obtaining a deliverance on that occafion, than on his
own prayers. Kenneth knew that his friend
was then at fea (as he probably let him know
of it, in order to have the benefit of his interceffion), and obferving the tempeft coming on
juft as he was fitting down to his meat, cried,
" It is not the time to eat when Columba is in
" danger;" and flew to the church in fuch
hafte, that though he had but one of his flip-

[5] Ad. iii. 15. In tuguriolo fcribens, fubito immutatur fa-
ciec, et hanc puro de pectore premit vocem, " Auxiliare,
" auxiliare !"—The danger of a monk in *Durrough* had prefented itfelf to his mind.

F

pers on, he would not wait to put his foot in the other. This was about the ninth hour; and very soon after, the tempest abated; which made Columba afterwards say, that they were obliged to Kenneth for not waiting for his shoes [6].

In order to excite men thus to pray for themselves, and intercede for others, he used to observe, that God's end in bringing his saints sometimes into danger, was to give an opportunity, and to excite themselves and others, to perform this duty with more frequency and greater intenseness. " Though *Colu-* " *man* the son of *Beogna* be just now in such " jeopardy in the eddying gulf of *Coire-* " *vrecain*, lifting both his hands to Heaven for " assistance, yet God will not leave him to " perish, his purpose being only to excite him

---

[6] Ad. ii. 12. Cognovi, o Cainniche, quod Deus tuam exaudiret precem,—valde nobis profuit tuus ad ecclesiam velox eum uno calceamento cursus. Kenneth died abbot of Achabo in Ireland, A. D. 600. One of the Hebrides near Iona, where he probably resided for some time, still bears his name, and has been lately celebrated in a beautiful Latin ode by Dr. Johnson.

" Parva quidem regio, sed religione priorum
" Nota, Caledonias panditur inter aquas.
" Voce, ubi Kennethus populos docuisse feroces
" Dicitur, et vanos dedocuisse deos," &c.
Boswell's Tour.

" to pray more fervently for his deliver-
" ance [7]."

Thus, in the moft unpromifing fituations,
he encouraged a truft in Providence, and cheered men with the hopes of deliverance from
their dangers, if they prayed and did not
faint. This truft he had in the higheft degree
himfelf, and expreffed the higheft fatisfaction
whenever he perceived it firmly fixed in the
heart of a difciple, " A huge fea monfter has
" been feen laft night in the courfe which you
" are to take to-day, my dear Baithen, and it
" may probably meet you." " And if it
" fhould," replied Baithen, " both it and I
" are in the hands of God." " Go in peace,
" my fon; thy faith is fufficient to fave thee
" from the danger [8]."

---

[7] Ad. i. 10. Columbanus filius Beognai nunc in undofis
Charybdis *Brecani*, &c. This dangerous gulf lies between
Jura and Craignifh.

[8] Ad. i. 19. This Baithen, the coufin, favourite difciple,
and immediate fucceffor of Columba as abbot of Iona, was
alfo much renowned for his wifdom, learning and fanctity.
In a very ancient account of his life (*ABa SS.* 9 Jun.), it is
faid that no man ever faw him idle, but always engaged in
reading, praying, or working: That, next to Columba, he
was deemed to be the beft acquainted with the Scriptures,
and to have the greateft extent of learning of any on this fide
of the Alps : That, for his zeal, prudence, fanctity, ftrict
difcipline, and primitive fimplicity of manners, Columba himfelf ufed to compare him to John the Evangelift : That he

F ij

The interceffion and prayers of the church,
or congregation of Chriftians, he efpecially recommended, and regarded fo much, that on
the greateft emergency, by night or by day,
he had always immediate recourfe to it [9]. Thus

was fo much given to prayer, that even in the neceffary intercourfe and converfation with his friends, his hands, though
concealed under his mantle, might be obferved to be every
moment lifted up to that praying attitude to which they were
fo much habituated : That whatever work he was engaged
in, his communion with God was fo clofe, and his attention
to prayer fo conftant, that he would not allow fo much time
as intervened between his fwallowing two morfels of meat, or
between his reaping a handful of corn and putting it in the
fheaf, to pafs without his putting up an ejaculation to Heaven ; and that his humility was fuch, that none could be more
careful to conceal his earthly treafures than he was to avoid
all oftentation of his heavenly graces.—After this account of
him, we need not wonder at his biographer hinting, that even
the devil was obliged to keep his diftance, and to leave the
diftrict of Baithen. On one occafion, however, we find him
peeping through the windows, to obferve whether each and
all in the family devoutly implored the bleffing of God upon
their meal before they began it, and folemnly returned thanks
when they had done.—If he ftill follows this practice (and
there is no reafon to think that he has flackened his diligence), he muft be highly gratified by feeing thefe matters
managed now pretty much in the way that he would wifh.

[9] Id. i. 22. Fratres intempefta nocte fufcitat Sanctus, ad
quos in ecclefia congregatos dicit, " Nunc Dominum intentius
" precemur—nam perpetratum eft peccatum, pro quo valde
" eft timenda judicialis vindicta."

Id. ii. 43. Fratres ad oratorium convocans, prefatur,—-
" Fratres, pro Cormaco orate, qui nunc patitur, &c.—nof-

when, on a certain day, he had notice of Aidan king of the Scots, one of his friends, being about to engage in battle, he quickly ordered the bell to be rung to fummon all his
monks to the church, in order to join their
united prayers for victory and fafety to Aidan [1].

Nay, the better to recommend the prayers
of the church, he afcribed to them not only
more efficacy than to thofe of any one faint,
however dear to God, but the power of almoft
changing the determined purpofe of God himfelf. One day, as two of his difciples talked
to him, they obferved his face brighten with
unufual and incomparable joy ; and in a moment after faw this placid and angelic fweet-

" tria commembribus compati debemus, et Dominum exorare
" cum iis."

[1] Id. i. 8. Sanctus—fubito ad fuum dicit miniftratorem,
" Cloccam pulfa." Cujus fonitu fratres incitati ad ecclefiam
ocius currunt—" Nunc intente pro Aidano rege et populo
" Dominum oremus," &c. Ufher refers this to the battle of
Leth-reidh, A. D. 590.—Columba judged, that when the
ftate protects the church, it owes to it, in return, its prayers,
and a ready co-operation in maintaining the good order of
fociety. St. Paul directed Chriftians to pray for kings and
rulers, when the king was Nero, and the rulers his cruel inftruments of perfecution. How much more fhould the church
obey the Apoftolic precept, when its kings and queens are its
nurfing fathers and *nurfing mothers* ?

nefs of countenance changed into grief and
fadnefs. With difficulty they extorted from
him the following account of thefe various appearances, on condition that they fhould keep
it a fecret till after his death : " Thirty years
" which I prayed God to give me in Britain,
" are now expired ; and I have much longed,
" and prayed, and hoped, that at the clofe of
" them I fhould obtain my difmiffion, and be
" called to my everlafting home with God;
" and juft now I was above meafure glad, on
" feeing the defcent of the holy angels to
" conduct my fpirit. But on a fudden they
" are ftopped at yonder rock ; for, the united
" prayers of the churches to fpare my life a
" few years longer, have prevailed over my
" moft earneft requefts, and changed the pur-
" pofe of God with regard to me. Four years
" more I muft remain on earth ; and then,
" without ficknefs or pain, this frame fhall be
/ " diffolved, and I enter into the joy of my
" Lord [1]."

---

[1] Ad. iii. 22. Facies mirifica et lætifica hilaritate effloruit,
oculofque ad cœlum elevans incomparabili repletis gaudio, &c.
" Angelos enim fanctos de excelfo vidi miffos throno.—Sed
" ecce fubito retardati—quia Dominus multarum magis ec-
" clefiarum pro me orationes exaudiens dicto citius immuta-
" vit," &c. Whatever the reader may think of fuch vifions,
he will be pleafed with the following fentence, in which Co-

It was the cuftom of Columba, to remark how, and when, God anfwered his prayers; and failed not, on fuch occafions, to acknow. ledge his goodnefs with praife and thankfgiving. Sometimes, too, he would call his friends to join him, efpecially if they had joined in the requeft. " God, my brethren, hath heard " the voice of our fupplication at fuch a time ; " he hath delivered our friends from danger ; " and it becomes us now to render to him our " united thanks [3]."

But what throws the moft beautiful luftre on this part of our faint's character, and fhows how much his pure fpirit was engaged in the high concerns of his miniftry, is, that even in his fleep, his mind, all awake, ufed to go on with the continuation of thofe prayers and interceffions which he had been urging at the throne of mercy through the day. When the

<hr/>

lumba defcribes the faculty of the *Seer* in language that would feem to have been dictated by experience : " Sunt nonnulli " quamlibet pauci admodum, quibus Divina hoc contulit gra- " tia, ut etiam totum, licet non femper, totius terræ orbem, " cum ambitu oceani et cœli, uno eodemque momento, quafi " fub uno folis radio, mirabiliter laxato mentis finu, clare et " manifeftiffime fpeculantur."

[3] Id. ii. 43. et iii. 13, &c. It is ftill cuftomary for perfons in diftrefs to afk the prayers of the congregation—I never heard a congregation afked, by any one, to return thanks for having obtained relief, but *once*. Compare Luke xvii. 15.

weakneſs of the body required reſt, the willing
ſpirit ſtill carried on the delightful work, and
pleaded the cauſe of his people with his God [4].

The prayers of Columba were not more remarkable for their frequency than for their
fervency, which was ſtrongly marked by his
attitude, voice, and countenance. His attitude, though he ſometimes ſtood, and was often
proſtrate, was commonly that of kneeling,
with his eyes raiſed up, and his hands ſpread
towards heaven [5]. From his extreme ſenſibility of heart, and earneſtneſs of ſpirit, his voice
was often attended with cries and tears [6]; and
devotion ſhone in his face with ſo vivid a lu-
ſtre, that the byſtanders uſed to aſcribe the
uncommon fervency and animation which appeared in it to ſome irradiation of the Divine
Preſence upon his countenance, as well as
upon his ſpirit [7].—Who can wonder if a buſi-
neſs called *the pleaſure of the Lord* proſpered ſo

---

[4] Ad. ii. 42. Noĉteque ſubſequenti (poſt nempe diem orationis et jejunii) ſanĉtus in ſomnio pro iis deprecatus eſt, &c.

[5] Id. iii. 16. Stantem et expanſis manibus ad cœlum, oculiſ-
que ad cœlum elevantem, &c. Id. iii. 13. Sanĉtus inter fratres pariter proſtratos, &c. Id. ii. 33. Flexis genibus, &c.

[6] Id. ii. 31. Flexis genibus et flebili voce, &c. Id. iii. 13.
Poſt intentam et lacrymoſam, &c. Id. ii. 43. Poſt orat. ab-
ſtergens lacrymos.

[7] Id. iii. 17. et iii. 23. et Cum. xii. Dum miſſarum ſolen-

aftonifhingly in the hands of a man fo zealous
and active, and at the fame time fo devoted to
prayer,—and to fuch prayer too as we have
been defcribing? To the minifter who thus li-
veth, and thus prayeth, all things are poffible.

So pious and devout a man as Columba,
muft have been poffeffed of a heavenly mind-
ednefs rarely to be met with. Accuftomed fo
much to be in company with God, and impreffed with fo lively a fenfe of the prefence
of angels or miniftering fpirits, he muft have
been deeply tinctured with their likenefs; and
in his temper and conduct refembled, while he
was yet on earth, the holy inhabitants of heaven [8]. Elevated as he was above every felfifh
and fublunary view, he had no end or aim but
to glorify God and to fave fouls. It is not
therefore without reafon that his biographers
compare him to one of the prophets or apoftles
of God [9], for he had no ordinary fhare of their
fpirit.

Befides, it has been already obferved that

---

nia ex more Dominica celebrantur die, facies venerabilis viri,
florido refperfa rubore videtur, &c.

[8] Ad. i. 1. Quamvis in terra pofitus, cœleftibus fe aptum
moribus oftendebat.

[9] Id. iii. 1. Quafi unus prophetarum Dei, inter ipfos con-
numerabitur—animarum dux innumerabilium ad cœlum. Id. ii.
33.—Apoftolicus homo.

G

Columba was defcended of noble parents, and
nearly allied to the royal families of both Scotland and Ireland; fo that he muft have had
large worldly profpects, if worldly profpects
could have allured him. Nay, he feems (from
his anfwer to Sigebert, to have been born not
only to large profpects, but to large poffeffions.
Yet of thefe, as of encumbrances retarding him
in his heavenly progrefs, he divefted himfelf,
by allowing them (as we are told by Odonellus) to devolve upon his three uncles; leaving
it to their own generofity to give him back
fuch portions as they chofe, in order to endow
his firft monafteries. Hence, when upon fome
occafion St. Ciaran was confidering whether
his own zeal for God was equal to that of Columba (for between thofe holy men this was
the only rivalfhip), he was humbled by a
dream or vifion, in which an angel feemed to
have fhown him an ax (an emblem of the profeffion of his father, who was a carpenter), fay-
ing, " This is what you have given up for the
" love of God, but Columba has given up a
" kingdom which was to have come to him by
" his father '."

The uncommon talents, education, and addrefs of Columba, would alfo qualify him for

---

' *Mag. Odonnel. Vit. Col.*

rifing very high in the fcale of worldly prefer-
ment, if this could attract him ; but inftead of
that, when actually offered him, it could not
divert him from the purpofe which he had already formed [2]. It would appear that he confidered the things of this world, both fmall
and great, as equally beneath his notice, except in fo far as they contributed to make him
more ufeful and holy, and to forward his progrefs to heaven.

Such was the eftimate which he feems to
have made of this world himfelf, and which
he laboured alfo to imprefs upon others ; teaching the fons of power and ambition, that even
a kingdom, if obtained at the expence of in-
nocence, was dearly bought, and could not be
long preferved : and exhorting thofe in hum-
bler ftations never to be greatly concerned a-
bout the frail and perifhing things of the prefent life. " Beware, I befeech you, my fon,"
faid he to a young ambitious prince [3], " that

[2] Omnem mundanæ celfitudinis gloriam afpernatus ; pa-
gum ratus fummos fecundum feculum honores ultro oblatos,
folo Abbatis munere contentus. *Id.*

[3] *Aodh-flan*, fon of King Dermit.—The counfel was thrown
away ; for he murdered *Sui'ne*, the fon of *Columan*, King of
Temora ; and in four years and three months after, the de-
nunciation here threatened had its accomplifhment, *Aodh* in
his turn being murdered by *Sui-ne's* fon *Connal. Ware.*

G ij

" you do not attempt to enlarge your poffef-
" fions by the commiffion of bloodfhed and
" murder ; for, if you do, God will foon de-
" prive you and your family of the inheritance
" of your fathers." At another time, feeing
one of his monks in great grief about a fmall
lofs which he had fuftained, " Why, my bro-
" ther," faid he, " fhould you be grieved on
" account of the lofs of fuch perifhing things
" as thefe *.?" And indeed, in this cafe, the
things loft were not the monk's, but Columba's
own; fo, that his exhortation or precept was
enforced by his own example.

Thus, in the eyes of Columba, heavenly and
divine things fhone always with fuch luftre as
to darken the brighteft objects of human ambition ; objects which he confidered, and reprefented, as often hurtful, rather than ufeful,
to thofe who attain the largeft fhare of them.
Hearing his fervant Dermit and another, who
travelled with him one day through the dreary
wilds of Ardnamurchan, fpeaking (probably
with fome envy) of the ftate of kings, and
talking particularly of *Beothan* and *Eachan*,
two joint kings of Ireland, " O my children,"
faid he, " how empty and unfatisfying are the

---

* Ad. ii. 39. Noli, frater, pro fragilibus contriftari re-
bus, &c,

" things you fpeak of; nay, how pernicious
" often are they to their owners; for the firft
" account you may probably hear of thefe
" kings, is, that their enemies have killed them
" for the fake of their poffeffions ⁵." On another day, as they were travelling towards Temora, he addreffed thofe who were with him
in the fame manner. " There is Temora,
" crowded with people, ftrong in military pow-
" er, abounding in nobles, and adorned with
" a royal palace, and filled with riches and
" ftores of provifion; but the time is approach-
" ing when it fhall be left defolate, a monu-
" ment of the inftability of human grandeur.
" Why fhould we love or admire the things
" that are tranfient and vanifhing ⁶?"
Indeed all his converfation generally aimed
at turning the thoughts of men from earthly
things, however great or defirable, to things
more durable and folid. Almoft every parti-
cle of it which is left upon record, and that is
not a little, favours of heaven and a heavenly
turn of mind. Its conftant tendency is, to e-

⁵ Ad. i. 12. On that very day they learned at *Lior-moir*
(Paradifus Muirbolc?) that this had actually happened; both
being flain by Cronen, fon of Tighearnagh, in the battle of
Glengevin, A. D. 572. *Ware*.
⁶ *Odonnel.* i. 84.

dify and profit as the cafe required, and as opportunity was given. And his condefcenfion,
affability, and aptnefs to teach, were fuch, that
he feemed never at a lofs to make every time,
and place, and perfon, fuit his purpofe. To
every perfon he had fomething to fay, by
which he infinuated himfelf into his favour,
and took occafion to edify him, in fuch a manner as fuited his exigency and capacity. If
he met but a child, he would afk whofe he
was, and give his benediction [7]. If in the
courfe of his peregrinations he had occafion to
meet a poor man, or perhaps to lodge with him
in his hut, he would begin perhaps with afking how many cows he had, and wifhing God
to blefs them to him till they fhould become a
large fold; and fo lead him by degrees to fubjects of higher importance [8]. If he fhould be
in the company of nobles or kings, he would
give the difcourfe a tendency either to make

---

[7] Ad. i, 10. Cujus eft filius hic ?—Sanctus benedixit, di-
cens, &c.

Id. ii. 20. Nefanus valde inops, Sanctum gaudenter hofpi-
tio recepit, miniftrans fecundum vires. Sanctus inquirit, Quot
boculos haberet ? Ille ait quinque. Ad centum crefcant—
et femen tuum benedictum, &c.

Id. ii. 22. De quantitate et qualitate fubftantiæ interrogat ;
et benedicens—" Deo donante habebis, &c.

[8] Id. i. 14.

themfelves good, as we have obferved above,
or to incline them to do good to others ; and
no other ufe do we ever find him making of
his great influence. Meeting one day with a
prince of the Orkneys, at the palace of King
Brude, he told the king, that fome monks had
lately failed with a view of making difcoveries
in the northern feas, and begged he would
ftrongly recommend them to the prince who
was then with him, in cafe they fhould hap-
pen to land in the Orkneys. They did fo, and
owed their lives to the recommendation of Columba [9]. Thus he would never negleft an op-

_____

[9] Ad. ii. 43. Such expeditions of the monks of Iona are
frequently mentioned by Adomnan. His late editor, Mr.
Pinkerton, thinks they were in queft of the Thule of the ancients, and obferves, that the Norwegians found Irifh monks
in Iceland when they firft difcovered it about the year 900.
Their objeft undoubtedly was, to difcover any land which the
gofpel had not yet reached, that they might preach to its
inhabitants the glad tidings of falvation. Nor were they lefs
zealous in roufing men to a greater regard for the truths of
the gofpel, by preaching it in its native purity and fimplicity,
where it was already profeffed. We meet with fome of them
in almoft every country in Europe, and their learning and
fanftity always procure them refpeft and honour. The number of them that went to France, Italy, and other foreign
countries, was fo great, that the Bollandine writers obferve,
that " all faints whofe origin could not afterwards be traced,
" were fuppofed to have come from Ireland or Scotland."
(*Vit. S. Blier.* 11 *Jun.*) The zeal of the monks of Iona is

portunity of turning the converfation to fome
purpofe that was ufeful, and of doing good to

---

diffeminating knowledge and true religion, in thofe dark ages,
is indeed aftonifhing. It flamed in the bofom of age, no lefs
than in the veins of youth. Cumian, at the age of 70, fet
out for Italy, where he became a bifhop ; and Coluŋman, afterwards bifhop of Lindisfarn (which he refigned rather than
change his way of keeping pafch) could not have fet out
for England from Iona, before he had arrived at the age of
80, as may be inferred from the account of his life by Colgan.
The account which Bede (iv. 4. et iii. 26.) gives of Columan and the other divines that went from Hii to England, is
interefting and curious. They inftructed a certain number of
the youth (e. g. Aidan had the charge of twelve) : They lived
in the moft plain and frugal manner, fupporting themfelves
by the labour of their hands, and folicitous only to improve
the heart : Except fome cattle, they had no wealth : If they
got any money from the rich, they immediately gave it to the
poor : Their houfes were barely fufficient for their own ac-
commodation ; for they never pretended to lodge or entertain
the rich, who had nothing to get from them when they came,
but the word of God, preached in the church. If the king,
with five or fix attendants, chofe at any time to take a re-
frefhment with them after the fervice was over, he muft have
contented himfelf with the plain and daily fare of the brethren.
Bede adds, that they brought religion at that time into fuch
repute, that a clergyman or monk was every where received
with joy as a fervant of God ; that when they travelled the
road, people ran to them to get their blefling ; and that when
they went to any village, which they did only when they had
occafion to preach, baptize, or vifit the fick, crowds gathered
to hear them. In fhort, fays he, the cure of fouls was their
great concern.

2

both the fouls and bodies of men. The converfation that was idle he difcouraged ftrongly,
though he did it gently, and alfo the mirth
that was unfeafonable and unbecoming [1].

From the notion which fome entertained of
his being able to foretel future events, a man
afked him one day how long he had to live.
If your curiofity on that head could be fatisfied, faid the faint, it could be of no ufe to
you. But it is only God, who appoints the
days of man, that knows when they are to terminate. Our bufinefs is to do our duty, not to
pry into our deftiny. God in mercy hath concealed from man the knowledge of his end.
If he knew it was near, he would be difqua-
lified for the duties of life, and if he knew it
were diftant, he would delay his preparation.
You fhould therefore be fatisfied with knowing
that it is certain; and the fafeft way is to believe that it may be alfo near, and to make no
delay in getting ready, left it overtake you un-
prepared.—Of another, who held a fimilar
converfation with him, he afked how long he
thought himfelf he had to live. The other replied, feven years. Confider then, faid he,
how much good may be done in fuch a fpace

[1] Ad. i. 12. O filioli, quare inaniter fic confabulamini, &c.
§ 43.—inutilia profertis verba.

H

of time ; but as you know not if it may be seven days, or even seven hours, it is now time to begin and to make ready[2].

So grave and serious was the constant tenor of his conversation, that it is said he was never obferved to have uttered an idle word, nor to have made the flighteft deviation from truth, even in joke or compliment. Odonellus relates that his difciple Baithen declared fo to king Aidan, and mentions one or two unfuccefsful experiments which were made by the king, to try whether the faint could be made to deviate from the ftrict account given of him by Baithen. Columba commanded the refpect of kings by fpeaking the truth, and the truth only, without ufing any idle words, compliment, or flattery. Aodh, king of Ireland, afked him, whether he thought he fhould be faved. You have little chance for that, faid Columba, unlefs you expiate the errors of your paft life by a fpeedy and fincere repentance, and by the exercife of good works for the future[3].

As the converfation of Columba was heavenly, fo his life and actions were alike ufeful and holy. Every thing he did was fuitable to his profeffion, and befpoke the *man of God*[4]. When

---

[2] Colgan. Vit. 5ta Columbæ.

[3] Id. ibid.

[4] Ad. i. 1. Opere fanctus.—ab omni integer labe. Id. iii. 23.

we confider his devotion, we fhould almoft
think he had left no room for activity; and when
we confider his ufefulnefs and activity, we fhall
almoft think that he had no time left for devotion. But they both harmonized fo fweetly,
that inftead of interfering they mutually ferved
to affift each other. And indeed the only way
to do much bufinefs, is to be much in prayer,
efpecially in the facred office. In any office,
to be good, and to do good, are but one and
the fame ftudy, though too many think they
may be feparately purfued. In Columba they
were both fo intimately united, that *holinefs
unto the Lord, and ufefulnefs to man*, were ftamped
on all his actions [5].

How much his character was marked with
the firft of thefe we have already feen, and the
other is equally manifeft, from his having been
conftantly engaged in doing all the good in his
power to the fouls and bodies of men. From

[5] Such was the fanctity and the ufefulnefs of Columba's
conduct that king Aidan, not being able to find in it any thing
that was either wrong or ufelefs, had the curiofity to afk him
(as Odonellus relates) whether he had fo much as any inward
motion or propenfity to fin? To this unneceffary queftion
Columba anfwered, as became a faint, that like all men, he
had fuch motions and propenfities; but that he would not
take the whole world, with all its honours and pleafures, and
confent to yield to one of them.

pure love to the fouls of men he gave up every
worldly profpect and profeffion, and fubmitted
to a life of the utmoft felf-denial, and toil, and
danger, and anxiety. With what activity and
zeal he laboured for the fouls of men, we need
no other evidence than the great and rapid
fuccefs of his miniftry. For clofe application
and activity he was indeed noted from his
early youth. When he ftudied under Finnian,
every night on which it fell to his fhare to grind
the corn with the *quern* or hand-mill, he did it fo
expeditioufly that his companions alleged that
he had always the affiftance of an angel in
turning the ftone, and envied him much on
that account. His future life is marked with
the fame clofe application and diligence⁵. He

<hr/>

⁵ From the early diligence and difpofition of Columba, his
mafter was enabled to predict his future greatnefs. Of the
many fcholars whom he had at the time, and of whom fome
made a great figure afterwards, he forefaw that none would
reach the fame of Columba. In a vifion of his, recorded in
the life of St. Ciaran, it is faid that he faw two ftars of extraordinary brightnefs. The one of them, which denoted
Ciaran, continued to fhine in its place; but the other, which
was by far the brighteft, moved towards Britain, but continued to enlighten Ireland as well as Britain with its beams.
This one, he faid, denoted the light of Columba's heavenly
doctrine, and his ardent charity and love to mankind. "Columbam, fulgentiffimum Hiberniæ et Britanniæ fidus, cœleftis
doctrinæ luce, aureo charitatis nitore, chriftallina puritate, re-
pleturum, &c." *Colgan. Trias.* p. 464.

flept little, was never idle, and never employed
about any thing that was uſeleſs [7], In a life ſo
buſy, and by a ſoul animated with zeal for the
glory of God and the ſalvation of ſouls, he hath
ſhown how much may be accompliſhed. His
zeal, like that of the *miniſters* above, was indeed
a flame of fire; ſtrong, active, penetrating
and cheering. It not only moved him to de-
vote his life to God, but to fill every moment
of that life with labour and action: infomuch
that with watching and praying, and the difcharge of the other various parts of his miniſtry,
he lived, to all the purpoſes of ſuch a life, more
in one day than ordinary paſtors perhaps in
many weeks or months. It is not by fitting
ſtill, and going through ſet exerciſes at ſtated
times, that miniſters can hope to make con-
verſions. Columba did not ſo make his. Un-
weariedly and inceſſantly we find him going
about, through his immenſe charge or diocefe,
from houſe to houſe, and from kingdom to
kingdom; and wherever he is, every word,
every deed, proclaims the faithful miniſter,
diffuſing every where the bleſſings of the goſpel,

---

[7] Vigiliis aſſuetus, ſomnique parcus; nunquam niſi actioni
alicui intentus; nunquam in actione otioſa vel inani repertus.
—Una actionum ejus omnium meta, Dei gloria, et animarum
falus. *Odonell. vit. Columbe.*

4

eftablifhing grace in fouls, and peace in families.

It has been already obferved that the faint
had always fomething fuitable to fay to every
perfon, of every age and condition. Yet he
feems to have paid the moft particular attention to the young; well aware of the importance of early piety, and of the greater probability of fucceeding in his endeavours to imprefs a fenfe of religion, when he had to work
on tender fouls. The young therefore he regarded with peculiar care ; encouraged them
to come to him on all occafions, and to fhare
in his inftruftions, prayers and benedictions [*].
Even before they were capable of learning,
he wifhed to cultivate their acquaintance and
to conciliate their favour, by the moft endearing tendernefs and condefcenfion ; that by
having their affections pre-engaged, he might
afterwards the more eafily convey his inftructions. Hence, when the faint makes his appearance, the little children rejoice to fee him,
and they run to meet him; and he embraces
them and takes them in his bofom [9]. If only
the elder children of the family fhould be prefented to him, he would fay, Have you not

---

[*] Ad. i. 10, 13, 16, &c.
[9] *Odonell.* ii. 10.

some that are younger than these ? I wish to
see them[1]. They are all sent for, and little
Eacban Bui (Fair-haired Hector), when he saw
the saint, ran up to him, and laid his head on
his bosom. The saint affectionately kissed him,
blessed him, hoped he would survive his father,
and afterwards leave children to succeed him.
How amiable is the saint when thus courting
the affections of children ! How lovely is old
age and holiness thus delighting to associate
themselves to infancy !

As the happiness of multitudes depends on
the temper and character of those who are
destined to fill the higher ranks of life, he attended more especially to such, had them often
with him, endeavoured to imprefs their minds
with a just opinion of worldly greatness, and to
infpire them with the love of peace ; the source
of long life to themselves, and of happiness to
those about them[2].

By this I mean not that Columba had any
respect of persons in any of his sacred ministra-
tions. In what related only to the individual,
and did not affect the interests of society at
large, the souls and persons of the lowest
shared in his labours and concern, as well as

---

[1] Ad. i. 9.
[2] Ad. i. 14. et i. 13.

thofe of the higheft. The family mentioned above, in which he fpent a day of fafting and prayer with a view to eftablifh peace in it, and about which he was fo anxioufly concerned, that his foul went on with the interceffion of the day during the fleep of the night, is mentioned to have been of the lower rank or plebeian order [3].

Columba indeed, like a true minifter of the Prince of Peace, and of that Gofpel which proclaims it, laboured for nothing fo much as to bring this blefling not only to families and to individuals [4], but even to kingdoms. In the great council of Drimceat, already mentioned, he mediated fo effectually between the Scottifh and Irifh kings, that both agreed to refer their refpective claims to his own decifion. This he modeftly, and perhaps wifely, declined, that he might not incur the difpleafure of either, but perfuaded them to refer the matter to Colman the fon of Comgel, a man " well verfed in facred and profane literature, and efpecially in the antiquities of Ireland." His great influence was in like manner exerted in preferving peace between the Scots and Picts, and in compofing their differences, when any

[3] Id. ii. 42.
[4] Id. ii. 16.—inter rufticanos—judicavit.

difference arofe. Equally refpected by both,
we find him going backwards and forwards
from the one court to the other, always zealous
and always fuccefsful in his endeavours to prevent or terminate the dire calamities of war.
Thus, by his great influence, he often faved a
torrent of bloodfhed both in Scotland and Ireland. The fame deference was paid to his
counfels in both kingdoms, and the moft mo-
mentous affairs often referred to his decifion.
Cairbre, the fon of Lugid Lamdarg, miffing a
ftroke aimed at a ftag, killed his brother;
which gave rife to a violent conteft between
him and a remaining brother, about the inheritance of the one that was killed. In vain did
the king and clergy of Ireland attempt to fettle
the difference. The contending parties, however, agreed to refer it to the decifion of Columba. They accordingly came, with a numerous
train to Iona, where the faint reconciled them,
and faved Ireland from a civil war. Happy would
it be for every age if the quarrels of kings and
kingdoms could be fettled, as they were then,
by being referred to fuch an umpire[1].

There was nothing about which Columba
was more anxious, or in which he was more

---

[1] Vid. *Annal. Ult.* 574. " Concio Drimaceat, in qua Columkil, &c. *Colgan. vit.* 5ta. *Beeth.* l. ix. et *Mag. Odon.* ii. 23.

fuccefsful, than in maintaining peace in all the
churches and religious focieties under his care;
nor was there any thing that feemed to give
him fo much concern as the apprehenfions
which he had that this peace might one
day be difturbed, by fuch foolifh difputes as
thofe which afterwards took place concerning
the feaſt of Eaſter². Columba however maintained the peace of the church in his day, and
with his dying breath left it in charge to his
difciples to have peace among themfelves³.

How ardently he loved peace may be inferred from its having been one of the three
things which, on a particular occafion, he is
faid to have folemnly afked of God, at *Tulach
nan Salm* (the Hill of Pfalms). The firſt was,
that he might never refufe any perfon in a
reafonable demand, left this fhould hurt his
ufefulnefs: the fecond, that the love and zeal
which he had for God in his heart fhould never
be abated: and the third, that all his friends
and relations might live in amity and peace
among themfelves; and, if at any time they
fhould not, that God would rather punifh the

² Ad. iii. 23. Multa, revelante fpiritu fanƈto, prophetavit
de illa quæ poſt dies multos ob diverſitatem Pafchaliæ Feſti orta
eſt inter Scotiæ ecclefias difcordia.
³ Id. iii. 23.

fault himself than allow them to hurt one
another [4].

But this love of peace in Columba never
hindered him from exercising the strictest difcipline and order; well knowing that without
this no lasting peace could be maintained. He
admonished and reproved with freedom, and,
when the cafe required it, with sharpnefs [5].
If that did not ferve, without any regard to
perfons, he proceeded to higher cenfures.
Thus, at the hazard of his life, he excommunicated some of the nobility of the kingdom
(the fons of Connel), after having first admonished and reproved them to no purpose [6].
Nay, when he faw no profpect of their reformation, after every mean of reclaiming them
was tried, he feems to have thought it mercy
to their own fouls, as well as to fociety, to requeft of God, if he had no purpofes of mercy in
referve for them, to fhorten the time of their
doing mifchief, and to check, by his Providence, the evil which could not be reftrained
by either law or religion.

These cafes, however, were very rare, and
extremely defperate, in which we find the faint

---

[4] Colgan. vit. 5ta.
[5] Id. i. 40, 41.
[6] Id. ii. 25.

proceeding to this laft appeal.—John, one of the excommunicated fons of Connel, continued to perfecute and harafs the good, and to live by rapine and plunder. Thrice had he robbed the houfe, and carried off the effects of a worthy hofpitable man who ufed to lodge the faint whenever he came his way. On the third time Columba met him as he was carrying off his booty, and earneftly entreated him to leave it. He followed him all the way to his boat (which lay at Camus in Ardnamurchan), and even waded after him into the fea with his fruitlefs petitions. The plunderer and his company (which feem to have been of much the fame caft with his followers on a former occafion, when one of them attempted to kill Columba) fcorned and laughed at him. The faint at length, lifting both his hands to heaven, prayed to God to glorify himfelf by avenging and protecting his people. He then fat down on an eminence, and thus addreffed a few who were along with him. " God will not always bear to have thofe who love and ferve him to be thus treated. That dark cloud already forming in the north, is fraught with this poor man's deftruction."—The cloud fpread—the ftorm arofe—and, between Mull and Colonfay, overtook and funk a boat, which no doubt the greed of plunder had too deeply loaded.—His fate, though juft (fo concludes with a tender concern the chapter), is much to be lamented [7].

If Columba was attentive to keep difcipline and order among his people, much more was he folicitous to do fo among his clergy. He feems indeed to have had nothing more at heart than to promote the purity and ufefulnefs of the facred order, and therefore he paid always the ftricteft regard to whatever related to their ordination and difcipline. He appears to have been not only careful to examine into their talents, views, morals, and earlieft habits of life, but even anxious to know if they were born of pious parents. He might probably reckon on fomething of the nature of the ftock being communicated to the fcion, as well as on the effect of good example, early difcipline, and timeous inftructions in piety. On this laft account he was particularly anxious to know if the mother, who has the firft moulding of the foul in the cradle, was herfelf truly religious and holy [8].

---

[7] Ad. ii. 23. Mifere quidem! fed digne.

[8] Ad. i. 17. Colgium [poftea primarium] de fua interrogat genetrice, fi effet religiofa, an non? &c. Plato, in like manner, makes it one of the requifites of a prieft, that he fhould be born of pious parents. Mothers efpecially have the firft forming of the mind, and if they are pious themfelves, it may

Whenever he difcovered any young perfons of parts and piety (in doing which he fhows great penetration[9]) he was particularly careful to cherifh them himfelf, to recommend them to others, and in due time to promote them, when their parts were well cultivated, and their piety well-proved. He himfelf ". was from his earlieft years inflamed with ardent zeal to attain to Chriftian perfection [1]," and he reckoned piety in youth to be the beft, if not the only fecurity for fanctity and ufefulnefs in riper years.

Of how much importance he thought it to have churches fupplied with fuch paftors as had been diftinguifhed for their early piety, appears from the earneftnefs with which, a fhort time before his death, he recommended to his fucceffor the care and promotion of a young man of whom he had juftly, on this ac-

---

be expected that they will do all they can to make their children pious alfo. On the mother it much depends, whether the children fhall, through eternity, have their portion with angels or with devils. How important is their truft! How folicitous fhould they be to difcharge it well!

[9] Id. i. 3. Hic puer, quamvis vilis videatur—bonis moribus et animæ virtutibus—fapientia quoque et prudentia crefcit,— et grandis eft futurus.—Hic, erat *Erneus*, poftea per omnes Scotiæ ecclefias famofus et valde notiffimus.

[1] *Odonell.* iii. 34.

count. conceived the higheft hopes.—" Take
particular heed, I befeech you, Baithen, to
what I am now to fay to you. After I fhall
be with Chrift, which I earneftly look and long
for. a youth of parts, piety, and ftudy, named
Finten, will readily come over from Ireland,
and make one of your monks. But I beg you
may not detain him here. Let him be the
father of a monaftery in Leinfter, where he will
faithfully feed the flock of Chrift, and lead .
very many fouls to glory [2]."

When any probationer had not turned his
attention to the miniftry till he was far advanced in life, an consequently wanted thofe
advantages which early habits of ftudy and
early devotednefs to the facred office might
furnifh, or when the character or qualifications
of fuch were anyhow doubtful, he was remark-
ably cautious of receiving them, till they were
long tried, and gave fatisfying evidences of
their fitnefs.—A man of this defcription came
to him one day from Connaught, requefting to
be put in orders. The faint, after fome quef-
tioning and examination, feemed rather defirous to divert him from his purpofe, however
well he might have thought of his intentions.
With this view he fet before him the ftrictnefs

[2] Ad. i. 2.

-of his monaftic *rule*, and all the hardfhips and labours to which the facred life was fubject. The candidate heard them all without being in the leaft ftaggered. Be it fo then, fays Columba: but before I adminifter the vows to you, I require of you firft to fpend feven years of probation in a monaftery to which I fhall fend you; that of Acha-luing in Ethica [3].

As he was thus careful himfelf about the piety, parts, preparation, and views, of thofe whom he admitted to the facred office, fo was he much grieved, and moved with uncommon indignation, when he heard of any unworthy perfon having been ordained or admitted to the miniftry by another. Being one day in-formed that *Aodh du' mac Sui'ne*, a man of high defcent, but a regicide, long inured to crimes, had profeffed to change his mode of life, and had been afterwards admitted into holy orders, he uttered the following dreadful fentence, which Adomnan delivers as a prophecy, and fays it

---

[3] Ad. ii. 40.—The long courfe of education and proba-tion required of his difciples by Columba muft have contri-buted much to their ufefulnefs, as well as to the fame which they acquired for learning, when the clergy of other parts of Europe were wofully ignorant. In the life of St. Munn, one of Columba's difciples, it is mentioned that his education took up eighteen years; in which there is no reafon to think that he was fingular.

was all fulfilled.—" Perifh the hand which *Finchan* laid upon that curfed head, and let it be dead and buried while himfelf is yet alive. As for *Aodh*, he will return to his former courfe of life, as the dog to his vomit, and be killed (as he did kill) by the edge of the fword[1]."

To preferve the purity of his monks, and indeed of all good men, he taught them, as a matter of the higheft confequence, to avoid as much as poffible the company and converfation of the wicked, when their charaëter was fuch as did not afford any profpeët of their being reclaimed: His own praëlice was to have as little intercourfe as poffible with fuch, any further than neceffity or piety required[2]. Obferving one day a man of this hopelefs ftamp about to land on his ifland, he immediately fent Dermit with orders not to allow him to fet foot on the ifle, but to fend him inftantly back to Mull[3]. On the other hand, he fo ftrongly recommended the company of the good, and urged fo much the advantage of having them always for affociates, that he a-

---

[1] Ad. i. 36.—Dermit I. of Ireland was killed at Rathbeg by this Aodh, An. 565. *Ware.*

[2] Odonell. iii. 42.

[3] Ad. i. 22 —Ne hujus infulæ cefpitem calcet.

K

scribed Cormac's want of fuccefs, in an undertaking of great importance, to his not taking
with him a man of much piety who wifhed to
attend him[4].

After what has been faid it is almoft unneceffary to add, that none ever fhowed greater
affection and regard to fuch of the facred
order as lived and acted according to the
fpirit of their office. To them he feldom or
never fpeaks without ufing the moft tender
and endearing names of brother, fon, or child,
or bleffed, or fome other expreffion of the
fame amount. But when he heard of any of
them being openly profane, or formal and
hypocritical in their profeffion[5], or inattentive
to the authority, dignity, and gravity becoming
their facred character, or countenancing and
giving their prefence to vain and idle amufe-

[4] Id. l. 6. The zeal of Columba's difciples to difcover
unknown countries, in which they might propagate the gofpel,
was noticed before; and for this zeal none was more diftinguifhed than Cormac, whofe voyages into the ocean are often
mentioned by Adomnan. Indeed all of them feem to have
the fame fpirit. One of them (St. Mochon) being urged by
his father to remain in his native country, replied, " You are
indeed my father, but the Church is my mother, and where-
ever I can reap the beft harveft, and do moft fervice to the
caufe of Chrift, that I confider as my country."—Odonell,
iii. 24.

[5] Ad. i. 35. et 21.

ments, though they fhould not otherwife fhare
in them, he failed not to denounce againft
them, above all finners, the heavieft judgments of heaven[6]. Such was his fenfe of
the fanctity of the office, his love for the
fouls of men, and his zeal for the fervice of
God, that he could never fee an unworthy
perfon in this office, without expreffing the
ftrongeft indignation. Seeing once an unholy
prieft officiate in celebrating the Euchariſt,
though he was not within his jurifdiction, he
could not help being moved fo far as to cry
out—Ah! what a combination of clean and
unclean things is here! the fymbols of the
facred oblation of Chriſt adminiſtered by
wicked hands[7].

It would be doing great injuftice to the
character of Columba not to obferve, that
though his zeal, at fome rare times, was thus
moved with indignation againft enormous vice,
or clerical profanenefs, yet he was habitually
a man of great meeknefs and fweetnefs of temper, who had brought all his paffions to fubjection, and ruled his tongue by the ftricteft
reins[8]. This, if we had no other evidence for

---

[6] Ad. i. 17. Si quando videris pincernam in cæna luden-
tem, &c. fcito te mox moriturum, &c.

[7] Id. i. 41.

[8] Linguam continuis cohibebat habenis. Odonell. iii. 41.

it, might eafily be inferred from the general
efteem and regard of all ranks for him, efpecially of his monks and fervants. This general
love and regard is feldom procured by the
feverer virtues, or even by good offices alone ;
they muft be accompanied by the fofter graces
of affability, meeknefs, condefcenfion, and
tendernefs. For, though we may give our
efteem to the former, we give our love only to
the latter; and thefe Columba poffeffed in a
very high degree. All perfons, rich or poor,
who had occafion to fee him, or even to folicit
him, in regard to the concerns of foul or body,
were fure of being received with a tender and
cordial embrace, of being treated during their
converfe with every poffible mark of benevolence, and difmiffed with the moft affectionate
farewell and benediction [9]. Every caution
which a deep concern for their welfare could
fuggeft, he would give before he could part
with them. " This day, I befeech you, my
fon, take not the ftraight courfe to Ethica [1], but

---

[9] Ad. i. 25, 18, 19, 20, 46, &c. Emigrantem ofculatus benediceret, &c.

[1] The Ethica fo often mentioned by Adomnan, is probably the Ifland Eig, or Eic ; *th* being mute in Gaelic, and *a*
but the Latin termination. It lay to the north of Iona, and
Baithen leaving Iona in the morning, with a fair wind, got to
Ethica before three o'clock in the afternoon. *Ad.* ii. 15.

rather fail round by the coaft and fmall iflands, for there are fome whales in the channel, and I cannot think of your being in fear or danger [2]."

Indeed, the near intereft which Columba took in every thing that concerned his friends was fo great, that he himfelf confidered it as a frailty. This amiable virtue, he thought, might carry off his attention too much from the contemplation and purfuit of divine and heavenly objects [3]. For, even when out of his fight, his friends and acquaintance were always prefent to his mind [4]; infomuch that if the wind but changed, he confidered how that change might affect them, and confequently how he fhould pray or praife in regard to them. " Fourteen days now has the wind been from the north fince Cormac left us. The danger to which he is driven, far beyond the reach of land, muft furely be extreme. Let us, my brethren, go all to the church, and earneftly intercede with God in his behalf." There, with bended knees and weeping voice,

---

[2] Id. i. 19.

[3] Natura fum fragilis, et carnalium amicorum et propinquorum amore frequenter occupor. Quanto enim plus inferiora, tanto fuperiora et cœleftia minus diligimus. *In Vit. Molar. Jap. Colgan.*

[4] Ad. ii. 43. Abfens corpore, fpiritu tamen præfens, &c.

he prays to Him who rules the wind; and
when it changes he gratefully returns to render thanks [5].

Towards his monks he always behaved with
such meeknefs and love, as endeared his perfon
to them fo much, that any of them would
willingly fave his life at the expence of his
own (of which an inftance has been already
noted), and perform whatever he defired,
though at the hazard of perifhing in the
attempt [6]. When he addreffed them, it was
always with the compellation of " brethren,"
or " children." When any of them offended
himfelf, he forgave him [7]; when any of them
offended God, he prayed for him [8]. His affection for them indeed was fo great that he
could hardly deny them any requeft, even the
moft unreafonable. When two of his monks,
on a certain occafion, wifhed to know the caufe
of that wonderful joy which they perceived in
his countenance, he ftrongly, but foftly, checked
their curiofity, and expreffed his extreme un-
willingnefs to difclofe what he wifhed to keep

[5] Ad. ii. 43. Flexis genibus et flebili voce Dominum
ventorum, &c.
[6] Id. ii. 28.
[7] Id. iii. 16.
[8] Fili, peccafti, et nifi ego orarem, &c.

fecret.—" Depart in peace, I befeech you, and do not urge me further about this affair." They clung to his knees, they wept, they humbly entreated him to comply.—" I cannot fee you fo fad, becaufe I love you, faid he, and will tell you, in the confidence that you will not, at leaft in my lifetime, reveal it [9]." Is not this the picture of a meek and tender parent, with his little children around him ?

Even his domeftics, or working monks and fervants, he generally addreffed by the tender compellation of " little children [1]," and inftead of reproving them for any fault which did not proceed from defign, would rather excufe and comfort them. One of them being ordered one day for Ireland, allowed the tide to carry away the leathern bottle (which he had for holding his milk) while it was fteeping within the fea-mark. His mafter faw his concern, and faid to him—My brother, be not concerned ; to-morrow, when the tide returns, we may probably find the bottle [2].

_____

[9] Ad. iii. 22.

[1] Id. i, 12—filioli, &c.

[2] Id. ii. 39.—Bottles were then made of leather, as in other places in ancient times. Yet it appears from Adomnan (ii. 34.) that they had then fome glafs utenfils, as he mentions the breaking of a glafs cup ufed for drinking. How

Towards Dermit, efpecially, his pious and conftant attendant, he difcovers on all occafions rather the affection of a parent, than the authority of a mafter. With what tender concern, for inftance, does he hang over his bed when he was thought at the point of death, and how earneftly does he requeft of God to heal and fpare his fervant Dermit, as long as he himfelf fhould remain in the prefent world [3]. His prayer was heard ; and for at leaft thirty-four years, to the honour of both, he and Dermit lived together, and we may believe that death could not long divide them.

---

they vitrified their walls in a much earlier period is more inexplicable. An inquiry into the ftate of the arts in the Highlands, in ancient times, and into the caufes of their decline afterwards, would afford matter for much curious inveftigation. The inquirer would probably meet with many facts that would lead him to fuppofe the population and civilization of the Highlands to have been in very ancient times fuperior to what they are even at prefent. It is at leaft 1590 years fince a royal palace in Argyllfhire, called Beregonium by hiftorians, and *Bailenrigh* (the king's town) by the natives, ceafed to be the refidence of kings ; yet, within thefe few years, a man who had been cafting peats befide it, alighted upon the pipe by which the water had been conveyed under ground to the citadel.—See *Stat. Acc. of Ardchattan.*

[3] Ad. ii. 30.—ad lectulum ftans—" Exorabilis mihi fias precor, mi Domine, et animam mei miniftratoris pii, de hujus carnis habitaculo, me fuperftite non auferas."

4

Every part of Columba's domeſtic character
is marked with ſenſibility and tenderneſs.
Even in the neceſſary labours impoſed upon his
monks, his feeling ſoul took a ſhare, and
miniſtered to them every conſolation in his
power. For this purpoſe would he viſit them
at their work, carried in a wain or wheel-car-
riage.[1], when by reaſon of age or infirmity he
could not go otherwiſe ; ſo that their joy and
happineſs in his ſervice was by themſelves
confeſſed to be greater than they could ex-
preſs by language. From the toil of the day
they always returned home cheerful and glad
at night, and from the love which they bore to
their maſter, they felt not the weight of their
burden. There is ſomething, ſaid one of the
oldeſt of them, which makes me ſo happy and
glad, that even when I am bearing this burden I do not perceive the weight of it [2].

[1] Adomnan has occaſion to make frequent mention of
chariots or wheel-carriages, and mentions it as miraculous, that
Columba had travelled in one for a whole day without the
wheel's having fallen off the axle, although, by neglect, it
had not been ſecured by the axle-pin. It is to be re-
gretted that Adomnan gives only thus ſome incidental hints
of the ſtate of ſociety in the time in which he lived. From
theſe, however, it appears that there has been a great falling
off at a later period.

[2] Id. iii. 23. et ii. 29.—et i. 37.—Veſpere redeuntes—unus
ex eis ſenior—Quoddam in tantum lætificat—ut me oneratum
non ſentiam.

L

For the monks of other monafteries, even
the moft diftant of his jurifdiction, he had the
fame tender regard, entered deeply into their
joy or forrow, grieving when they were grieved,
and rejoicing when they rejoiced. On a certain winter's day, which was exceffively cold,
the faint was obferved to be in the utmoft
diftrefs, and even to weep bitterly. His fervant, Dermit, took the liberty to afk the caufe
of his forrow, and got the following anfwer :—
" It is not without reafon, my child, that I am
this day fo fad. My monks in *Durrough* are,
at this inclement feafon, fadly oppreffed by
Laifran, who keeps them at hard labour to
build him a larger houfe."—Soon after he
learned that Laifran had relented, and put a
ftop to the work till the weather fhould be
milder ; upon which he rejoiced exceedingly,
communicated the glad tidings to his brethren,
and bleffed the relenting heart of Laifran [3].

---

[3] Ad. i. 29.—Laifran, or Lafran, " a man of zeal," was
the name of feveral faints and monks.   One of them is called
hortulanus, and *hortularius*, " the gardener."   Many of thofe
faints employed themfelves occafionally in practifing and teaching ufeful arts as well as fciences ; taking every method to
make themfelves acceptable and ufeful in order to benefit and
civilize mankind.   Hence fome of them are defigned by the
arts which they occafionally taught and practifed.   One of
the St. Ciarans is called *Saighr*, or " the carpenter ;" and St.

The tendernefs and fenfibility of Columba
were indeed exquifite, and eafily interefted

Senach is denominated *Faber*, " the fmith," or rather " a
maker of iron;" as may be inferred from a paffage in Odonellus,
in which he is faid to have been, on a certain occafion, employed in melting and forging that metal (" liquendis cuden-
difque ferramentis occupatus"). This gives fome probability to
the current tradition, that the Highlanders poffeffed the art of
making their own iron; that the flag or drofs frequently to
be met with on the mountains, marks the ftance of their
forges; and that the pofterity of thofe artifts are thofe who
ftill bear the furname of *Mac-an-Fhuibher* or *Mac-an-Fhaibher*
(Lat. *Faber*), and call themfelves in Englifh MacNuier and
MacNair; the *fb* and *bb* being mute in the Gaelic words.

Of what fciences were taught in Iona, befides divinity, we
have no particular account. But as Columba was himfelf well
fkilled in phyfic, we may believe that he would not fail to
teach his difciples a fcience that would contribute fo much to
their ufefulnefs. The *Olla Ileach*, and *Olla Muileach*, the ancient and famous line of phyficians in Ilay and in Mull, muft,
no doubt have derived their firft knowledge from this feminary.
I had from Major Maclachlan, in the neighbouring ifland of
Luing, a MS. in the Irifh character and language, on the
fubject of medicine and furgery, which appeared, from being
compared with Aftle's fpecimens, to have been of a moft remote antiquity, and it is moft likely that it was written by
fome of the learned men in Iona. That they ftudied the
laws, cuftoms, and hiftories of nations is plain, from their
having been the perfons whom Aidan carried with him to the
council of Drimkeat, to vindicate his title to his throne
(upwards of 100 of them, according to *Odonellus*, iii. 2.
having accompanied him for that purpofe), and alfo from the

L ij

him not only in what concerned his friends and domeftics, but any part of the human race however diftant. One evening, as one of the monks came to fpeak to him after grinding the corn, he obferved his mafter's countenance (which always ufed to be ferene, cheerful, and pleafant) fo full of terror and concern, that he ran haftily back, greatly alarmed, and unable to account for fo extraordinary and unufual an appearance. After a little time, however, he took courage, went back, and requefted to know the caufe. The faint told him that he had juft learned that a city of Italy was deftroyed by lightning, by which above 3000 fouls had perifhed [*].

To thofe who were nearer hand, Columba gave more fubftantial proofs of his regard than outward figns. He difcharged every focial duty with the utmoft care, doing good to all, and giving caufe of offence to none. His

---

claims of the rival kings having been referred to St. Columba, and when declined by him to St. Colman Eala, who has the character of having been " well verfed in facred and profane literature, and particularly in the antiquities of Ireland." How well they ftudied the languages appears from the excellent Latin of Cumin, and of Adomnan, who difcovers alfo his knowledge of Greek and Hebrew; and wrote a geography of the Holy Land.

[*] Id. i. 28.—Suppofed to be Civitas Nova, *Notker in Martyrol.*

caution in this laſt reſpect was extremely great. His monks had one day cut ſome ſtakes and wands to repair their houſes, of which, perhaps, the ſides as well as roof were made of wicker, or wands woven on ſtakes [5]. The poſſeſſor of the ground from which they were taken was ſomewhat diſpleaſed, although ſuch things were at that time, and for ages after, conſidered as no man's property, and indeed of no value · in a country over-run with wood. Yet the ſaint, when he heard of it, could not bear to have any man offended, and therefore immediately ſent him a valuable preſent of barley for ſeed, and to enhance its value, and ſhow his benevolence, he ſent his benediction along with it [6].

---

[5] Such houſes were afterwards plaſtered with clay, and made no uncomfortable habitations. Adomnan mentions that a celeſtial light was ſeen to dart through the key-hole of a houſe in which Columba had been privately praying ; from which it may be inferred that the houſe had no other chinks in it, otherwiſe this would not be particularly mentioned. The reaſon that we ſee ſo few remains of buildings prior to the uſe of lime, is, becauſe many of them were conſtructed in this manner. Some buildings however of very remote antiquity were built in the moſt ſufficient ſtyle. The walls of one of theſe erected on the promontory of Kintyre, are above eleven feet in thickneſs ; for what purpoſe it is difficult to ſay.

[6] Ad. ii. 3.

In every fhape, indeed, his benevolence exerted itfelf towards all within his reach, and moved him to compaffionate alike the fouls and bodies of men. If they were in prifon, he vifited and comforted them [7]; if in bondage, he redeemed them [8]. Silver and gold, it is true, he had not often ; but what he had he cheerfully gave away. A valuable fpear, embellifhed with ivory, is the price of one ; and

---

[7] Id. i. 11.

[8] Id. ii. 40. et ii. 34. Slavery is utterly inconfiftent with the fpirit of the gofpel; and fo hoftile to it was Columba, that, contrary to his ufual practice, he not only refufed to give medicines to a mafter that was fick, but alfo affured him that his difeafe would foon prove fatal, if he did not accept the condition upon which he offered his affiftance, and give liberty to his female-flave, which till then he could not prevail with him to do. Of flaves or captives there feem to have been but a few inftances in the jurifdiction of Columba, and his zeal in their behalf muft have foon procured their liberty. We do not find that this kind of flavery prevailed afterwards in the Highlands. In Ireland it did ; and Giraldus Cambrenfis (i. 18.) fays, that at a general convocation of the clergy, &c. in 1170, the calamities which the Irifh then fuffered, were afcribed to their having been in the practice of buying flaves from England, partly ftolen, and partly fold by their parents ; and that it was then ordained that all the Englifh flaves in Ireland fhould have their liberty. Colgan, who cites the paffage, wifhes that the Englifh would, in their turn, follow this example ; left, as they were deeper in the guilt, their punifhment would be more fevere.

reftoring the fick mafter to health is done on
condition of obtaining releafe to another: contrary to his ufual practice of giving his trouble,
fkill, and medicine freely ⁹. For, whenever he
heard any was in ficknefs, he not only vifited
him, and prayed for him, and that too with
fuch tender emotion as fhowed how much his
heart was affected ¹, but alfo adminiftered medicines, with which he often fent meffengers
as far as other kingdoms ².

When the ailments of his patients were of
fuch a nature as to allow them to travel, he
encouraged them to come and ftay with him,
that he might be the better enabled to underftand their difeafes; and that, if he could not
reftore them to health, he might at leaft prepare them for dying. The value of an immortal foul, capable of everlafting happinefs or
endlefs mifery, he knew to be inconceivably
great; and the right improvement of the few

⁹ When the rich, however, chofe to make him prefents on this account, he did not refufe them. We find
one of the kings of Ireland, on the recovery of his fon, re-
warding Columba with 30 head of cattle; and another of
them, on a fimilar occafion, makes him a gift of lands for
building and endowing the monaftery of *Drim-cliabh*. *Odonell.*
i. 56, 60.

¹ Id. ii. 31, 32.

² Id. ii. 4, 5.

precious moments allowed by Heaven for its
próbation, to be a matter of unfpeakable confequence. If, therefore, he might help any one
whofe moments of grace had not yet expired,
to form one good purpofe, perform one good
deed, or if he could excite one pious fentiment
in their foul, he knew it would be of more value than if he could give them a kingdom.
Such opportunities, therefore, as conferred the
power of doing this, he eagerly fought for;
and when the duty of refidence (with which
he feems unwilling to difpenfe but when the
reafon was great and urgent) did not permit
his going from his charge at home, he wifhed
to have thofe who approached near their end
brought where he was.—Go, faid he to two of
his monks, to the cell of *Diun*, at Loch-ava, and
tell *Cailtan* to make no delay in coming hither.
Cailtan came, and the faint told him, that as
he underftood his life, was near a clofe, he
wifhed to have him with himfelf, that, as a
lover and friend of his foul, he might help him
to finifh his courfe with the greater comfort [3].

Such was the hofpitality of Columba, that,
without being fent for, any one might come,
and affuredly rely on being made welcome,
not only for days, but for months or years, if

---

[3] Ad. i. 31. He died within a week.

this were to do him fervice[1]. Two ftrangers, on a certain Sabbath day[2], cried on the other fide of the little frith that feparates *Hy* from Mull. Make hafte, faid Columba, and bring the ftrangers over. They came ; the faint faluted them ; and having inquired into the caufe of their coming, they told him that they came with an intention to remain with him during that year. The faint probably perceiving that their ftate of health would not permit them to live fo long (as he hinted to fome others), recommended to them to enter into the number, and to commence the life of monks. They did fo, and died within the fpace of a month.

Hofpitality, in a country thinly inhabited, and in a rude ftate of fociety, is a virtue of the firft order. Columba therefore recommended it ftrongly by his preaching, and en-

---

[1] Id. iii. 7. Peregrinus ad fanctum perveniens, per aliquot apud eum menfes in Hyona commanebat.

Id. i. 32. Ut hoc anno apud te peregrinemus venimus.

[2] Perhaps the circumftance of its being the Sabbath day, is mentioned in order to fhow that Columba preferred the exercife of mercy to the obfervance of a pofitive precept; as he himfelf fet fo ftrict an example of obferving the Sabbath, that when he travelled, he always remained wherever the fun went down upon him on Saturday evening, till it rofe on Monday morning (*Colgan.* p. 410.). Without a due obfervance of the Sabbath, fmall muft be the influence and effect of religion.

M

forced it by the fanction of promifes and threats [3], but more efpecially by his own example; without which the preacher muft always preach in vain. Befides, Columba's manner of difcharging this duty, and his attentions to his guefts, were fuch as greatly enhanced the merit of the performance. Before the guefts have yet arrived, he orders the water to be got ready for bathing their feet, to refrefh them after the fatigues of the journey [4]; and, like a true minifter of that religion which prefers mercy to facrifice, he diffolves even the folemnity of a faft, for the fake of difcharging the duty of hofpitality to the weary and hungry traveller [5].

Columba's own regard to hofpitality, and its vaft neceffity and value in fuch places and times, may account for the high indignation which a man of fo meek and mild a fpirit ex-

---

[3] Ad. ii. 20, 21. [4] Id. i. 4.

[5] Id. i. 26. This faft is faid to have been on the 4th day of the week (or Wednefday), and called " the cuftomary faft;" whence it appears that they kept on this day a weekly faft; a practice which, Colgan fays, continued in the Irifh church till the beginning of laft century when he wrote. The day obferved by the Romifh church was Friday. Adomnan calls the days of the week by their ordinal number after the LORD's day; not by their Roman names.

preſſed upon an occaſion on which its ſacred
laws were moſt atrociouſly broken, and the
crime complicated with murder. Taran, a
Pictiſh exile of noble deſcent, was anxiouſly
recommended by the ſaint, for a few months,
to the care of a powerful man in Ilay, of the
name of Feradach; who, inſtead of protecting
as he promiſed, ordered him, after ſome few
days, to be put to the ſword. The ſaint, who
probably conſidered himſelf as accountable for
the exile, ſoon heard of his having been murdered by Feradach, and thus gave vent to his
emotion :—" It is not to me, but to God, that
the poor unhappy man hath lied. His name
ſhall be blotted out of the book of life. It is
now midſummer, and in autumn, before he
ſhall have taſted the fleſh of his hogs, after
they ſhall have fed upon the nuts, he ſhall ſud-
denly die, and ſuffer the juſt reward of his
crimes."—Feradach hoped to belie the prophecy, by procuring the earlieſt nuts, and kil-
ling a boar which ate of ſome of them, before
the uſual time. But on the very day, or rather
at the very inſtant, when it was juſt brought to
him, and when he thought to have taſted of
it, according to Adomnan, he fulfilled the pre-
diction [6].

---

[6] Ad. i. 24   Extenſam manum, priuſquam ad os conver-
teret, expirans, mortuus, retro in dorſum cecidit.

This, and one or two fimilar denunciations
in the life of Columba, will be afcribed by
fome to a prophetic impulfe, and by others to
a fpark of paffion, ftruck, even out of a fancti-
fied heart, by the collifion of a very ftrong
provocation. Accordingly, fome will perhaps
place them to the fcore of merit, and others to
that of ·defect or foible. I fhall only obferve
that whatever may be thought of thefe inftances, Columba's ordinary and habitual frame
of fpirit was of the moft placable and forgiving
nature. Few, if any, ever gave him more
trouble or oppofition than the Pictifh prieft, or
Druidh, Broichan[7]. Yet when he heard, as he
travelled near his place of refidence, that this
man was thought to be a-dying, he made all
poffible expedition to heal him[8]. And though
it is well known that the bards, in Columba's
time, were become a nuifance to fociety in

---

[7] Broichan had the merit, however, of dealing in a more
open and avowed manner than fome of his brethren. Odonellus (ii. 11.) relates, that when Columba firft landed in Iona,
on Pentecoft eve, fome druids who had been there, difguifed
themfelves in the habit of monks, and pretended they had
come to that place to preach the gofpel, with a requeft that
he and his followers might betake themfelves to fome other
place; but that Columba immediately difcovered the im-
pofture, and that they refigned the field to him.

[8] Ad. ii. 34.

general, and extremely adverfe to the views of thofe who propagated the Chriftian religion, yet at the great council of *Drimceat*, when all the other members unanimoufly agreed upon their being put to death, and an end being put to the order, Columba alone interceded in their behalf, and by his great influence the bards were faved [9].

---

[9] O'Conner and O'Flagberty, cit. ap. Pink. in Ad. i. 50. The bards from their connection with the druids, whofe fuperftition was to be fet afide, were very troublefome to the firft preachers of Chriftianity, fome of whom were not difpofed to fhow them the fame charity with Columba. Poor St. Colman was fo provoked by them as to wifh at length that the earth might fwallow them as it did Korah and Abiram (*Vit. S. Colm.* 7 Jun.). But Columba was not only fond of their poetry (*Ad.* i. 42.), and a poet himfelf, but of a different fpirit; though he too was often teazed by them. Odonellus mentions one occafion on which they threatened to lampoon him for not giving them, when at the time he had nothing about him to beftow : and fuch was his tender regard for his character, that he was obliged to wipe the fweat from his face with his hand, before he got clear of them. Afterwards, however, they were very grateful for his interceffion in their favour; and Dallan, the chief of them, exerted all his fkill to praife him. When he had recited but a part of the poem to the faint, who feemed to be much pleafed with it, Baithan, fearing that even his mafter might be elated with the praife, as well as pleafed with the poetry, put him upon his guard, by telling him that he faw a black cloud of *cacodæmons*, or evil fpirits, hovering over his head. Columba took the hint, ordered the poet to ftop, and never to repeat the poem after-

When the injury or provocation was directly offered to himfelf, he was equally ready to forgive, and even to return his enemies good for evil. A thief had gone from Colonfay to Mull, with a view of carrying away fome of the faint's property on a fmall adjoining ifland [1]. Before he could get off, he was difcovered, apprehended, and brought to the faint, who thus addreffed him: " Why do you thus go on in the practice of ftealing your neighbour's goods, and breaking the commandment of God? For the future, come to me whenever you are in need, and you fhall have what you have occafion for."—At the fame time he ordered fome wedders to be killed and given him, that he might not return empty to his poor family. And learning foon after that he was not likely to live long,

---

wards; adding, that no man fhould be praifed until he had reached the goal and finifhed his courfe. Dallan waited till Columba did fo; and then publifhed his poem, which was well known in Ireland till very lately (if not ftill) by the name of *Ambra Cholum-chille*, or the Eulogy of Columkille. *Colgan.* p. 432.

[1] Ad parvam infulam, ubi marini noftri juris vituli generantur et generant : ut de illis furtim, fuam replens naviculam, &c. It is to be regreted, that Adomnan did not tranfmit the knowledge of the now unknown art by which Columba was able to make a property of feals or fea-calves, fo as to put it in the power of any one to fteal, or fill his boat with them,

he ordered a fat' mutton and fix meafures of corn to be fent to him; which, as he died about the time in' which the fupply arrived, ferved the occafion of his funeral [2].

It is only in thofe cafes in which finners were paft all hopes of reformation that Columba gave them up: and even then, his fevere fentence might be uttered. as the laft effort of a gracious fpirit to roufe and to reclaim them. If, after all, finners went on and died impenitent (an event which we cannot fuppofe his threatenings would haften), no man could be more grieved. The fevereft groans that ever broke from his heart, were thofe to which he gave vent, when he heard of finners having died in their impenitence [3].

But when any perfon repented of his fins, none could poffibly fhow more regard and tendernefs. On the top of the eminence above his monaftery, Columba fat one day, looking out moft anxioufly for the appearance of a fail from Ireland. Dermit was near him; and to him he expreffed his concern at not feeing a veffel which he expected to arrive on that day, with a man who had fallen into

[2] Ad. i. 42.

[3] Id. i. 44.—Gemitu ingemuit mœfto—quod mutuis vulneribus transfixi, &c.

some grievous sin, for which he now laboured
under the sincerest sorrow and repentance.
Dermit soon after told him that he perceived a
sail making towards the port. Then, said the
saint, let us quickly rise and meet the penitent; for Christ himself receives the penitent.
Fechnus landed; Columba ran to embrace
him; mingled his tears of joy with the tears
of sorrow shed by the other, while he thus
addressed him : " My son, I beseech thee take
comfort; the sins which thou hast committed
are forgiven; for it is written, *A broken and a
contrite heart God will not despise* [4].

In speaking of the benevolence and tender-
ness of Columba's heart, we must not omit his
charity in relieving, and procuring relief for,
the needy, by every method in his power [5];
besides praying for the blessing of God to in-
crease their store [6].

In one of the accounts of his life, published
by Colgan, we are told, that after he had
erected the monastery of Durrough, he ordered
a hundred poor persons to be served with
victuals every day at a certain hour, and appointed an almoner for that purpose. One
day a mendicant came to apply for a share of
this charity, but was told by the almoner that

---

[4] Ad. i, 30. [5] Id. ii. 38. [6] Id. ii. 20.

3

he could have nothing, as the appointed number had been already ferved. He came the
fecond day, and was told in like manner that
he was come too late, and that for the future
he muft come earlier, if he expected his fhare
of the charity. The third day, however, he
came as late as before, and when the almoner
gave him the fame reply as formerly, he bade
him go and tell from him to the abbot that he
ought not to limit his charity by any precife
rules which God had not prefcribed, but
always to give while he had, in whatever
number, time, or manner, the poor fhould
apply to him. Columba, upon receiving this
meffage, ran haftily after the mendicant, who
had then affumed a heavenly form; which
gave him to underftand to whom he was indebted for the counfel. From that day forward he laid afide his rules, and gave to all
objects, at all times, provided he had any thing
to beftow. If at any time he had not, his
tears would flow, till God enabled him to relieve their wants. Hence, adds the writer,
he was efteemed, what he really was, the
common father and patron of the poor and
needy[1].

Next the falvation of fouls, the object which

---

[1] *Colgan. Trias.* p. 377 et 438.

moſt engaged the heart of Columba was charity. St. Mobith, who had juſt built a church,
brought St. Ciaran, St. Kenneth, and St. Columba to ſee it, and deſired each of them to
ſay with what things he would have it filled,
if he had his wiſh. Ciaran, who ſpoke firſt,
ſaid he would wiſh to have it filled with holy
men ardently engaged in celebrating the
praiſes of God. Kenneth ſaid his wiſh would
be to have it filled with ſacred books, which
ſhould be read by many teachers, who would
inſtruct multitudes, and ſtir them up to the
ſervice of God. And I, ſaid Columba, would
wiſh to have it filled with ſilver and gold, as a
fund for erecting monaſteries and churches,
and for relieving the neceſſities of the poor.
And to you, ſaid Mobith, God will give the
power to do what you now wiſh to perform [2].

Even Baithen, who had ſo much of the ſpirit
of his maſter, thought that Columba ſometimes
rather exceeded in the exerciſe of alms-deeds,
or charity. One day as the reapers were employed in cutting the corn, Baithen came
home before them to ſee if their victuals were
ready, and was much diſſatisfied at finding
that Columba had given to the hungry the
moſt of what had been made ready for the

reapers. But his mafter, with a mild and tranquil voice, told him that God would repay with intereft whatever was given away for his fake, and that he would find that what remained would, with God's bleffing, be enough to fatisfy the reapers [3]. .

Of all Columba's virtues, indeed, none was more confpicuous than charity [4]. He never faw any man, in any diftrefs, without doing all he could to relieve him; and nothing grieved him more than to fee a rich man void of charity to the poor; an evil which he laboured fo much to cure, that on one occafion we find him refufing to partake of a rich man's entertainment, till he brought him to a fenfe of his fin in this refpect, and to a promife of amendment [5].

His deteftation of avarice is ftrongly marked by an incident recorded by Odonellus. Two mendicants, the one noted for his careful, the

---

[3] Id. p. 411.

[4] Sed inter reliquas omnes ejus virtutes fingularis prærogativa charitatis et mifericordiæ facile principem locum tenuit. Neminem uquam in aliqua corporis vel animæ neceffitate conftitutum intelligebat, cui, qua poterat, ope vel opera non contenderit fubvenire. Cum laborantibus laborabat, cum infirmantibus infirmabatur; cum flentibus femper, et cum non flentibus fæpe flebat. *Ibid.* p. 437.

[5] Ad. i. 51.

other for his diffipated turn of mind, applied
to him at the fame time for charity. To the
firft he gave a little money, but to the laft a
great deal more. Some who were with him at
the time, expreffed their difapprobation at his
giving moft to the one who, in their opinion,
was the leaft deferving. Columba defired
them to inquire what ufe each made of what
he gave them. They did fo, and found that
the firft, who happened to die immediately
after, had put up what he got with ten pieces
of gold which he had fewed in his garment;
while the other had taken the firft opportunity
of fpending what he had got, and giving all
about him a liberal fhare of what he had pur-
chafed [6].

In any of the facred order, efpecially, he was
fo fhocked at feeing a want of charity to the
poor, or that avaricious and tenacious turn of
mind from which it fprings, that this made
one of the rare provocations, which, as already
obferved, made him lofe the calm tenor of his
foul, and, for a moment, give place to the
feelings of an indignant fpirit.—*Gallan*, one of
the clergy of your diocefe, faid he to Bifhop
Colgion, I underftand is juft now dead. His

---

[6] Mag. Odonell. iii. 53. See Poem againft Avarice, in the
Appendix.

heart was hard and avaricious; and his foul is now with devils [7]."

On the other hand, he fhowed the higheft regard, and gave the warmeft commendation, to every perfon of diftinguifhed charity. Here, faid he on a very public occafion, is the gift of a rich man who has mercy for the poor; and therefore, mercy fhall eternally reward his bounty [8]. He was particularly delighted when at any time he difcovered a high degree of this amiable virtue in a man of mean or ordinary circumftances.—In the inland parts of Scotia [9], fays Adomnan, lived *Colum Coilrin*, a fmith by occupation, remarkable for his virtues, and above all, much given to alms-deeds and cha- rity. In an advanced age he died; of which Columba, having got immediate notice, thus fpoke to thofe who were with him at the time: " Happy man! who, with the labour of his hands, hath obtained from God fuch eternal rewards in heaven: for, whatever he could make of his trade, that he gave to the poor in

---

[7] Ad. i. 35. [8] Id. i. 51.

[9] When Adomnan wrote, Scotia or Scotland was one of the names for Ireland, which afterwards came to be appropriated to this country, when the Scottifh nation had attained to con- fiderable power in it, after their return from Ireland, into which they had been driven by the Piǎs.

charity. And now his foul is conducted by
the holy angels to the glory and joy of the celeftial paradife'."

Compaffion, indeed, was fo ftrongly marked
on the foul of Columba, that he was difpofed,
on all occafions, to exercife it, not only to his
own fpecies, but to every creature under
heaven. Some perfon had once the prefumption to requeft of him to blefs his dagger.
" God grant then, faid the faint, it may never
fhed a drop of the blood of either man or
beaft²."

The following incident will further illuftrate
this part of Columba's character: A crane had
one day taken its flight acrofs the feas from
Ireland, and, by the time it drew near the
fhore of Iona, was fo fpent that it was obliged
to alight in the water. The faint forefaw that
this was likely to be its fate, and had already
ordered one of his monks away, though it was
at the moft diftant part of the ifland, to take
up the poor bird, and fave its life. Bring it,
faid he, to the neareft houfe, feed it, and take
all the care you can of it for three days, till it
be well refrefhed, and recover its ftrength, fo
as to be able to crofs the fea again to its native
home. The monk obeyed, and the faint was

---

¹ Ad. iii. 9.   ² Id. ii. 30.

thankful.—" For this act of mercy and hofpitality, may God command on thee his bleffing,
my dear brother."—" What a beautiful picture (fays the late editor of Adomnan) have
we in this chapter of the benevolence of Columba ³."

Another incident of the like nature occurs
in the account which we have of the tranfac-
tions of the faint's dying day ⁴. He had been
to fee and to blefs the provifion of his monks,
from whom he was on that day to be taken
away. On his return to the monaftery, he fat
down on the way to reft him. His old white
horfe, which ufed to carry the milk veffels betwixt the monaftery and the fold, obferved
him, came where he was, reclined his head
upon his breaft, and, as if fenfible of his
mafter's near departure, began to exprefs his
grief by groans, and even tears. Dermit
offered to turn him away, but the faint for-
bade : Let him alone, faid he, let him alone,
for he loves me, and I will not hinder him on
this occafion to drop his tears in my bofom,
and fhow the bitternefs of his grief. To thee

³ Pinkerton in Ad. i. 49. The title of this chapter in Adomnan is " Of a certain circumftance which, though fmall, ought
not, I think, to be overlooked."—Pity if it had, for it is
owing to thofe fofter tints that pictures charm us.

⁴ Ad. iii. 23.

God hath given reafon; but fee (that they might not be defpifed), he hath planted affection even in brutes; and in this, even fomething like a prefcience of my departure. Now, my faithful and affectionate friend, be gone, and may you be kindly cared for by Him who made you!

It is with particular pleafure I obferve in how high a degree Columba poffeffed another and higher fpecies of charity than that which I have been fpeaking of; I mean the liberality and candour of his fentiments, in allowing a fhare in the manfions of the bleffed to the truly virtuous of every perfuafion. When men, unenlightened by the gofpel, lived according to the light of nature and of confcience (dim as it was), God, he believed, would accept them for their having improved the talent which they received, without exacting of them any account of the talent which they received not. The honeft Heathen, who had a difpofition to receive the gofpel, if he had a tender of it, obtains at his difmiffion, like the Chriftian faint, a convoy of holy angels. Travelling one day along the fide of Lochnefs, and having got intelligence of a worthy Heathen in the neighbourhood being at the point of death, he made no fcruple to fay to thofe

about him, that the angels were already come
down from heaven to conduct the soul of that
man to glory. At the same time he did not
think it unneceffary, at leaft not improper, to
haften his pace, and if he could overtake it,
give him an opportunity, which he probably
heard the man had wifhed for, of being initi-
ated into the Chriftian faith by baptifm [1].

It deferves to be noticed, as a matter very
congenial to this candour of foul, that Columba is faid to have forever maintained a cheerfulnefs of countenance, and an angel-like
afpect [2], which ftrongly attracted the love of

---

[1] Ad. iii. 14.—A fimilar inftance is mentioned (i. 33.) of a
a man in Sky, " naturale per totam bonum coftodiens vitam,"
&c. This man, who appears to have been a ftranger, and probably a Roman officer (primarius cohortis), landed here by fome
accident, is the only inftance in which we find Columba ufing
an interpreter; fo that it is highly probable the northern Picts
ufed, with perhaps fome difference of dialect, the fame language with the Scots. In moft cafes we find the conquerors,
being the feweft in number, have adopted the language of the
conquered.

[2] Id. i. 1.—Afpectu angelicus,—hilarem femper faciem
oftendens.—J. Tinmuthenfis, in his account of Columba (ap.
Colgan. p. 332.) makes this a part of his fhort, but compre-
henfive character of him (afpectu angelicus, fermone nitidus,
opere fanctus, ingenio perfpicax, et confilio magnus), " his
countenance was angelic, his fpeech elegant, his conduct holy,
his underftanding clear, and his defigns magnificent."

O

the beholder, and at the ſame time ſhowed how much his ſoul was filled with that heavenly joy which is the fruit of the Spirit, and the preſent portion of the genuine ſons of God [3]. Some may perhaps think that the auſtere and mortified life which Columba led was inconſiſtent with this cheerfulneſs of aſpect and joy of ſpirit. But if we make a due allowance for the difference of the times, the force of this objection will entirely be removed. His ſleeping on the bare ground, for inſtance, with a ſtone for his pillow, was no extraordinary mortification for a monk, when the luxury of the rich could afford, perhaps, but a little ſtraw [4]. Beſides, it was prudent for him to inure himſelf from choice to thoſe habits of life at home, to which he muſt have generally ſubmitted from neceſſity when he travelled abroad. The life of Columba was indeed mortified and ſelf-denied, but had in it nothing irrational or unmeaning; nothing that looked like ſuperſtitious penance, or tormenting himſelf with unmeaning hardſhips.

---

[3] Ad. i. 1. Sanctorum ſpecie, ſancti ſpiritus gaudio in intimis lætificabatur præcordiis.

[4] Feather beds, however, were not at that time unknown. That of Roderick king of Strath-Clyde is mentioned. *Plumatiuncula;* lectulus plumis confertus. *Du Cange.*

Accordingly, one of his biographers obferves, that notwithftanding his auftere and toilfome life, by which he was much fpent and extenuated, yet he was comely in his drefs and outward appearance, of a florid countenance and cheerful afpeĉt; infomuch that he looked like one who lived in a nice and delicate manner[5].

Ufelefs and oftentatious aufterity he avoided himfelf, and difliked in others. Hence, we find him fharply reproving a perfon who, by way of doing penance, affeĉted to impofe upon himfelf hardfhips which neither God nor his fpiritual guides required[6]. He looked upon

---

[5] Odonell. iii. 43.—Exteriora forma et corporis habitu fpeciofus, genis rubicundus, et vultu hilaris, quafi homo in deliciis enutritus, femper apparebat.

[6] Ad. i. 21.—From the title and firft line of it (*Colgan.* p. 472.), it would appear that one of Columba's Irifh poems was intended to correĉt fome miftakes of this nature.

"Fioruifge maith a ciall maith a tuigfe."

"From the Fountain of Truth nothing can flow but what is agreeable to reafon and found judgment."—The writers of the *Aĉta SS,* (ii. 233.) have therefore much miftaken the meaning of a phrafe in Adomnan (iii. 16.), of Columba's going out to pray "in hiemalibus," though they might have underftood it from the fubftantive fupplied in the next page of their edition "hiemali noĉte." They underftand it of the praĉtice of fome faints, efpecially of Britain and Ireland, who ufed to fubdue the body with the rigours of cold, by praying at night in the midft of ice and fnow, and even immerfed to the neck

every part of religion as a pleafure, and practifed it from choice, not as an impofed tafk or
burden. No wonder then if it filled his heart
with joy, and his countenance with gladnefs,
for this is always its genuine, effect on every
one who rightly underftands its doctrines, and
fincerely obeys its precepts. This is, befides,
the moft effectual means to recommend our
holy religion to others who are yet ftrangers to
its power. Yes, cheerfulnefs is, indeed, *the
beauty of holinefs*, and contributed no doubt to
Columba's acceptablenefs and ufefulnefs, in
conjunction with his affability, tendernefs, and
lowlinefs of mind; for lowlinefs of mind or
humility fhone in the character of Columba as
much as any other quality, though he did not
at any time affect or make a fhow of it [7].

He was not only eafy of accefs to all who
came for either charity or inftruction, as alfo
affable and cheerful, as became one who was
filled with fo much inward joy, but fo humble

in cold water. This fafhion, which never prevailed much,
has paffed away. But it may ferve to make us think how
little we do, for what others did fo much. If they erred on
oné extreme, let us take care that we do not err upon another;
which is more dangerous.

[7] Q. Marg. and K. David of Scotland, ufed to wafh the feet
of fix beggars every night to exercife and fhow their humility;
not confidering that if the proud or evil fpirit thus went out of
one, he muft have entered into *fix*.

as to condefcend to the meaneft fervice by
which he could do good, and to take a fhare
in grinding the corn, and other manual labour
of the monks. The preference to which he
was entitled he never affumed, being always
difpofed to think lefs highly of himfelf than of
others [8].

The greateft faints are always the moft
humble: a truth of which this man is an
inftance; although he had more temptation to
pride than moft men of his own or any other
age. Courted, vifited, and loved by all the
petty kings and princes of Scotland and Ireland [9]; revered and almoft adored by the
great body of their people, who crowded the
roads where he travelled, and brought their
gifts to entertain him where he lodged [1];
obeyed by armies of monks in both kingdoms;
and his company fought after by their bifhops
and abbots [2], who, without any mark of envy
or emulation, acknowledged his vaftly fuperior

[8] Omnibus neceffitatis vel utilitatis caufa accedentibus fe
colloquio affabilem, benignum, jucundum, et interioris lætitiæ a
fpiritu fancto infufæ indicia hilari vultu prodentem, fe femper
exhibebat. Tantæ erat humilitatis ut in manuali, &c. *Odon.*
iii. 42. et 39.
[9] Ad. iii. 5. et i. 15. et i. 10.
[1] Id. i. 51.
[2] Ad. ii. 13. et iii. 17, &c.

merit—what fuel was this to inflame his pride,
if the laſt ſpark of it had not been quite ex-
ftinguiſhed! But we find Columba the ſame
meek and lowly man to the very laſt, and ſo
little uplifted with all the honours that could
be done to him, that upon an occaſion on
which a whole country poured out to meet
him, and ſurrounded him with hymns of joy
and ſongs of gladneſs, his whole attention is
taken up with a poor boy, whom he had
fingled out of the crowd, on account of ſomething in him which he thought a promiſing
fign of piety and future uſefulneſs, On what
might glorify God or benefit man his thoughts
were intent, and not on the glare of the triumph [3].

Of modeſty, a virtue near akin to humility,
Columba's biographers frequently obſerve that
he had an uncommon ſhare. The Office for
his Feſtival ſays, that virgin-modeſty was one of
the particular graces given him by God; and
Odonnellus ſays, that his modeſty was ſuch
that he could hardly look at any woman
directly in the face [4]. Nor is it improper to

---

[3] Id. i. 5. .

[4] It deſerves to be remarked, that notwithſtanding this
modeſty of Columba, none could be bolder in the diſcharge of
his duty; in doing which he feared not the face of man,

obferve that this modefty is remarked to have been one of the guards by which the avenue of the eyes was defended againft the entrance of any illicit thought that might infect his pure mind : for without ftrictly guarding the avenues of the fenfes, even faints ought not to prefume on being fecure from temptation. Columba, zealous of angelic purity and evangelic perfection, watched thefe doors with diligence, that nothing might enter in to hurt himfelf, nor fo much as an idle word come out to hurt another. Perhaps fome may think his caution was exceffive, and that his vigilance and labour both were more than were necef--fary. His own anfwer to fome who told him fo was, *For, every idle word we have an account to render.* He who does not ftrive fhall never be crowned ; he who does not run fhall never win the race. To enter heaven requires all

---

When, by impofition of hands, he conftituted Aidan king, he not only told him his duty plainly, and charged him to obferve it, and to teach his children in the fear of God to do the fame ; but alfo denounced the heavieft judgments againft him and them if they did not. " In that cafe," faid he, " the lafh which I endured from the angel, on thy account, fhall be laid upon thee, and the fceptre fhall be wrefted from the hands of thy children." *Cumin* et *Ad.* iii. 5.

our exertion, and can never be expected by
the fecure and indolent [5].

From fpiritual pride Columba was fo free,
that he avoided mentioning any of thofe fpecial vouchfafements which were made to his
foul: or if the importunity of any who chanced
to difcover the effects of them, extorted from
him a reluctant account of them, it was under
promife or oath that as long as he lived they
fhould fay nothing of the matter [6]. And
though no man was more inftant or earneft in
prayer, he is ready to afcribe the favours
which he receives, not fo much to his own
prayers for them, as to the prayers of others [7].
How amiable is fuch humility, and how well-
becoming every follower, and efpecially every
minifter, of the meek and lowly Jefus! And
how incompatible is pride with their character,
with their office, and with their ufefulnefs.

With pride, or even pomp and magnificence
in any clergyman, Columba had no patience;
nor could he fee it without being moved with

***

[5] Nemo dormiens coronabitur, nemo fecurus poffidet regna
cœlorum, &c. *Offic. S. Col.* et *Odonell.* iii. 41.

[6] Id. iii. 7.—Nullo modo in hominum notitiam paffus fit—
ut jactantiam devitaret, &c. Id. i. 44. Sancti et Apoftoloci
viri vanam evitantis gloriam, &c.

[7] Id. ii. 12.

indignation and denouncing its downfal. Obferving one day a man driving his carriage
along the plain of *Bres*, in much ftate, and
only intent on his amufements, he afked who
he was; and being told he was a rich clergyman, he replied, " He may be fo now, and
enjoy his amufement and pleafure; but he is a
poor man, indeed, on the day on which he
dies[1]." To fee a clergyman depart from the
gravity and fanctity of his character, or pafs in
diverfion and idlenefs the time that fhould be
devoted to the duties of his calling, is what
Columba, with all his meeknefs, could never
bear. So awful, in his opinion, was the nature
of the facred character and office.

After fo large an account of Columba's life
and character, it may be expected that fomething fhould be faid of his doctrine. A man
of fo much concern for the fouls of men, we
fhould naturally fuppofe to be faithful in de-
claring to them the whole counfel of God.
And for this his early education, and unwearied perfeverance in ftudy rendered him
peculiarly qualified. His paffion for ftudying
the fcriptures, efpecially, was moft intenfe,
when the other parts of minifterial duty
allowed him to indulge it. Thus we find him

---

[1] Ad. i. 39.

P

fometimes engaged for whole days and nights
in exploring dark and difficult paffages of
fcripture, and accompanying his ftudy and application with prayer and fafting [2].

Hence, Columba, and his difciples for feveral
generations, had a clearer and better knowledge of the gofpel than moft of their contemporaries, and taught it to the people in its
native purity and fimplicity. With the errors
which at that time prevailed in the Church of
Rome they feem not to have been in the leaft
tainted [3]. Columba, inftead of fubmitting to
the fpiritual tyranny of that church, withftood
her errors, borrowed his monaftic inftitutions
from fome Eaftern churches, and declared that
only to be the counfel of God which he found
in the fcriptures. It was by proofs produced
only from them, that his conduct was directed
and his doctrine confirmed [4]. The venerable

---

[2] Ad. iii. 18,

[3] Mr. Pinkerton juftly obferves, that till the end of the 9th
century, Iona was the Rome of Scotland; and we may add, of
at leaft a great part of Ireland. See *Appendix*. That Columba
fhould have kept clear of the errors which prevailed in his
time is the more remarkable, as Odonellus fays he vifited
Rome in perfon, which may be alfo implied in the Office for
his Feftival, in which he is celebrated for having vifited diftant
places; and of thefe the chief at the time was Rome.

[4] Ad. i. 22,—" Prolatis facræ fcripturæ teftimoniis," was

Bede, with all his zeal for the Church of Rome, allows the divines of *Hü* (or Iona) to have poſſeſſed the higheſt knowledge of divinity, and acknowledges · how much the churches throughout ·Britain were indebted to them, for their preaching the goſpel ſo zealouſly, and accompanying it with ſuch purity and ſimplicity of manners[5]. At the ſame time he laments how long they wanted the only thing which, in his opinion, they needed in order to be perfect—the rites of the church, eſpecially the right knowledge of the Paſch and Tonſure[6].

---

the rule by which he taught his diſciples to ſupport their doctrine.

[5] How the miſſionaries from Iona were qualified to preach the goſpel (as Bede tells us) to the Saxons, or people of England, who had a different language, is a matter that requires to be explained, and points out, perhaps, a method which in ſuch caſes deſerves to be imitated. To accompliſh their object, they brought ſome Saxons to Iona, from whom they might learn the language of the country to which they were going ; as well as educate them for returning, when fit for it, to teach their countrymen. Thus we find Adomnan mentions ſeveral Saxons in Iona, ſuch as St. Pilo, a Saxon; St. Gueren, a Saxon ; and a Saxon baker, or *piſtor* (*Edit. Pinkert.*) which the editions of the Bollandines, Colgan, and other Catholics have printed *pictor*. But as Columba had no images, he had no occaſion for a painter.

[6] Bedæ, Hiſt. iii. et v. 23.—Qui inſulam *Hii* incolebant monachi ut gens ‾quæ noverat ſcientiam divinæ cognitionis,

If St. Palladius and St. Patrick, who preached
the gofpel in Ireland before St. Columba, were
fent by the Pope of Rome, as many authors
affirm, it is probable that Columba may'have
differed in fome points from thofe who taught
before him ; and for this difference of opinion,
which might lead him to rejeĉt the traditions
and ufurpatïons of man, it was perhaps owing
that' he ran the hazard of being excommunicated before he left Ireland, notwithftanding
the holinefs of his life, which his opponents.
themfelves confeffed to have fhone as a light
from heaven [7]. This intended indignity, how-

_____

populo Anglorum communicare curavit.—Domino curante
poftea ad ritum Pafchæ et Tonfuræ perduĉti funt.—Ut ad per-
feĉtam vivendi normam. pervenirent.—The Nicene council, in
the 4th century, had decreed that the Pafch fhould be celebrated " in Dominica poft decimam quartam lunam, norr in
ipfa luna decima quarta.:" but the Monks of Iona adhered
long to their old regulations, and their crime was " quod
fanĉtum Pafcha luna decima quarta celebrarent, fi· forte· hæc'
in Dominica caderet ; cum, eo cafu, lunam vigefimam primam
expeĉtare debuiffent!"—In regard to the Tonfure, the Ro-
manifts affeĉted the form of à crown, and reproached thofe
who differed with them, with having got their form from
Simon Magus. Every age has its folly, and every age fees
the folly of the paft without adverting to its own.

[7] Ad. iii. 3.—Adomnan does not mention the caufe, but
calls it trivial ; and Odonellus gives the following account of
it, which is perhaps more curious than fatisfaĉtory. Columba being on a vifit to St. Finnen at Drimfionn, got a

ever, was foon compenfated by the veneration
paid him by all ranks of people, in that as
well as in other kingdoms.

It is a curious fact in hiftory, though not fo
generally known as it deferves, that a large
body of paftors and people in the ifles and
mountains of Scotland, like the Waldenfes
among the Alps, maintained the worfhip of
God in its fimplicity, and the gofpel in its

---

book from him to read, with which he was fo much pleafed,
that he fat up for fome nights to take a copy of it ; which,
when he had done, Finnen would not allow him to take with
him, but infifted on having the copy returned along with the
original. To avoid any difpute, both agreed to refer the
matter to Dermit king of Ireland; who decided in favour of
Finnen, in the following words, which have fince become
proveibial, *Le gach boin a beiniom, le gach leabhar a leabhran,*
" To every cow belongs its calf, to every book belongs its
copy."

Soon after, a war having broke out between Dermit and the
king or prince of Connaught, the former was worfted, and a
great many of his people flain, in the battle of Culdremin
(A. D. 561.). As the leaders of the Connaught party were
the near relations of Columba, the victory was afcribed to his
fuppofed prayers in their behalf; which excited againft him the
general indignation of the king and clergy on the other fide :
to avoid which, it is faid, he immediately refolved, with the
advice of St. Mael-Jos, to leave the kingdom. *Odonell. et Vit.
SS.* ii. 196. As we do not find Columba's influence was
leffened in Ireland, the true caufe of his leaving it muft have
been his zeal to extend his ufefulnefs.

purity for many generations, when it was greatly corrupted in other places [a]. A change, much for the worfe, began to take place among them about the beginning of the 9th century, when almoft all the monks of Iona were deftroyed or difperfed by Danifh free-booters, and when thofe misfortunes commenced, which afterwards endured for ages. Society was unhinged by war, anarchy, and defolation; and a feminary of learning, in fuch a ftate, could not be expected to ftand [b]. Yet fome of the good feed feems to have been ftill preferved and propagated in the country, by the Culdees, fprung from the fchool of Columba [c].

---

[a] " In the early ages of the Chriftian church, the Highlands and Iflands of Scotland were the feat of learning and religion : of religion that was not derived from the church of Rome, as appears from their differing from it about the time of keeping Eafter, and feveral other things. Icolmkill was then a feminary of all kinds of learning, and a nurfery of divines for planting churches.—In England, with great zeal, many of them taught and propagated religion out of the prophetic and apoftolic writings." *Dr. Cumming's Serm. et aut. cit. Ranulphi Polichronicon, Gale, et Warner Eccles. Hift. of England.*

[b] See *Chron.* in Appendix.

[c] " In fome of our iflands which we are now apt to confider as the feats of ignorance and barbarifm, lived a people remarkable for fimplicity of manners, purity of behaviour, and unaffected piety ; and thefe were the little leaven which

But we return to Columba, and obferve, that although he did not at any time depart from the purity of fcripture, he feems to have been at great pains to drefs its doctrines in fuch a form as was moft likely to engage the attention of a people who, like all uncivilized nations, were much more accuftomed to indulge their imagination than to exercife their judgment. Several inftances of his thus dexteroufly accommodating his reprefentations of Divine truths to the circumftances and capacities of his hearers, may be obferved in the account of his life by Adomnan. The monks, for inftance, in the firft period of their inftitution, had uncommon trials to encounter, and were to exhibit to the world a higher degree of fanctity and mortification than other men. They, therefore, were to be cheered with higher rewards and brighter profpects. *The faints fhall rife firft*, was a text which naturally fuggefted a prior refurrection to the monks, to whom the appellation of faints

---

afterwards leavened the whole lump. Of their number was Columba, &c.—Even in the 10th age, when the darknefs of corruption and error had greatly increafed, we are told there were fome godly men in Scotland, who taught the true doctrine of Chrift's atonement, and continued to exercife their functions apart, without acknowledging the authority of thofe who affumed a fpiritual power over God's heritage."
Bonar's Serm.

was more peculiarly, though not exclufively, appropriated: and to have a fhare in their refurrection was the firft object of ambition, and the promife of it a fource of fpecial confolation [2].

Befides this, as many were in thofe barbarous times called forth to fuffer and to die for the caufe of God, and needed every help to make them encounter any form of death with cheerfulnefs, the innocent expedient was devifed of affigning to the martyrs a feparate burying-place, where their facred duft was never to be contaminated with that of ordinary men. To fleep in this holy of holies, ftill known by the name of the *Martyr's Cemetery* [3], was to faints themfelves an object of defire.

We know that angels conduct the fpirits of the juft to heaven; and Satan being prince of the power of the air, their way muft be through his dominions; fo that a conflict between two fuch oppofite powers may naturally be fuppofed [4]. By an obvious and lively figure

---

[2] Ad. ii. 40.—Cum meis monachis in refurrectionem vitæ de fomno mortis evigilabis.—Qua a fancto accepta—non mediocri confolatione valde lætatus, &c.

[3] *Clagh nam Martireach.*

[4] See on this fubject, *Scot's Chriftian Life.*—In the fculpture on the pillars of the cathedral of Iona, is ftill to be feen the reprefentation of Michael and the Devil weighing fouls in a balance.

of fpeech an animated preacher might, on the death of an acquaintance, reprefent this conflict as if he faw it, and defcribe its probable iffue, fuitably to the character of the departed; efpecially if it was decidedly marked as very good or very bad. Columba, whofe fancy was lively, fometimes fat thus in judgment on the dead, in order to excite the living to virtue [1].

When faints, after fo many intervening dangers, were thus brought fafe to heaven, it was natural for the church on earth to celebrate the triumph, and to rejoice at the happy tranfit and deliverance of a departed member of their body. Accordingly, on fuch occafions, Columba convened his monks, fung hymns, adminiftered the Eucharift, and praifed God for his mercy to the foul of a brother [2]. And

---

[1] Ad. ii. 6, 11, 13.—Quorumdam juftorum animas crebro ab angelis ad fumma cœlorum vehi, fancto revelante fpiritu videbat : fed et reproborum alias ad inferna a dæmonibus rapi fæpenumero afpiciebat. Ad. i. 1.

Hac enim nocte præterita, vidi fubito apertum cœlum, angelorumque choros S. Brandani animæ obvious defcendere, quorum luminofa et incomparabili claritudine totus eadem hora illuftratus eft mundi orbis.

Chrifto gratias ago, quia victores fancti angeli, contra, &c. animam hujus peregrini cœlo receperunt. Cumin. 4.

[2] Ad. iii. 11, 12.—" On a certain day as the brethren were making ready in the morning to go out to the different works in which they were to be employed, Columba told them

Q

if his life was remarkable for fanctity and
ufefulnefs, this, as it were his birth-day, was for
the future obferved as a holiday as oft as the
year returned. This cuftom, which in thofe
times was pretty general, had the ftrongeft
tendency to promote holinefs of life, and to
make the virtuous look forward with joy to
the day on which they were to have the happinefs of dying.

Farther, as angels are miniftering fpirits, and
the faints faid to be after death *as angels*, fo Columba reprefented the departed faints as being
tenderly concerned for their furviving friends,
and employed to perform the office of angels
to their fouls, at the time of their departure
from the body.—" Happy, happy woman, faid
Columba (on occafion of the death of a pious
woman), this moment the angels convey thy
foul to paradife !"—Next year her hufband,
who was equally pious, died alfo.—" What joy
muft it give him now at his departure," faid
Columba, " to be met by the foul of his wife,
together with holy angels, to bring him to the

they were to keep that day as a holiday; that they fhould
prepare for celebrating the Euchariſt, and make fome addition to their little dinner, as on the Lord's day, out of refpeɛ
for the foul of St. Columban, bifhop of Leinfter, whofe foul
was laſt night carried by choirs of angels to the paradife of
God beyond the ftarry heavens." ·

manfions of the bleffed·³!"—Death, attended
with the lively belief of fuch pleafing circumftances, had in it little to be feared ⁴.

From thefe inftances we may eafily perceive
that Columba was ·at great pains to prepare
and fuit his manner of teaching to the exi-
gencies and capacity of his hearers, by giving
fpiritual doctrines, as it were, " a·body and a
local habitation ⁵." And it deferves our no-

---

³ Id. iii. 10.

⁴ The example, as well as the doctrine, of thofe holy men,
helped to ftrip death of its terrors, and to make it more than
welcome to the beholders. A country man who had come to
fee St. Aed on his death-bed, was fo ftruck with what he faw
and heard, that he immediately threw himfelf into the fame
bed, where he lay with the faint, till both died together.
Vit. Aedi.

As Columba himfelf rejoiced at the profpect of death, fo
alfo did his difciples. St. Odhran, one of the twelve who
firft accompanied him from Ireland, finding himfelf unwell
foon after he landed, expreffed his defire that his foul might
be foon with Chrift, and his body the firft pledge that fhould
confecrate Iona to his companions. " My dear Odhran,"
faid Columba, " fhall have both his wifhes; and they who
fhall hereafter afk for my tomb, fhall next inquire, Where is
Oran's ?" *Odonell.*—Accordingly *Relic Orain* is ftill fhown to
ftrangers.

⁵ Sometimes we find Columba teaching by actions inftead
of words. As he and Baithen had been walking on the fhore,
they faw a boat finking, by which feveral perfons perifhed.
After lamenting their fate, and obferving that one of them
was very wicked, Baithen afked how God allowed the in-

tice, that after all his pains and preparation, he was so fensible that his sufficiency was not of himself, that he seems to dread the difcharge of the moft ordinary part of his public functions, without previous prayer for the Divine affift- ance. Before he adminifters the ordinance of baptifm, we find him retiring firft to a private place to pray ⁶.

Having this high fenfe of the importance of his public miniftrations, it is no wonder if he performed them with animation and fenfibility. From this, his warm and affecting manner, and from the extraordinary alacrity and joy with which he difcharged every part of his duty, may have proceeded, in part at leaft, thofe wonderful accounts already mentioned, of the irradiation of his countenance, as if it fhone,

nocent to be fometimes involved in the punifhment of the wicked ? Of this Columba feemed to take no notice till they came to a bee-hive ; in examining which, one of the bees ftung Baithen, upon which, with a fweep of his hand, he killed it with feveral more. Why, faid his mafter, did you kill the innocent with the guilty ? I fuppofe it is becaufe they were in bad company.—Columba embraced every op- portunity of turning every incident to the purpofe of edifica- tion. " There is a poor woman gathering wild herbs for food. Are we not afhamed to fee fome take more pains to preferve a perifhing life, than we do to obtain that which is eternal ?" *Odonell.*

⁶ Ad. ii. 9.

on fome occafions, with a glorious and heavenly
luftre, when he was engaged in the celebra-
tion of the holy ordinances of religion. This
account of the matter may perhaps be allowed
by thofe who are unwilling to afcribe it (with
Cumin and Adomnan) to the prefence and
manifeftations of angels.

After having difcharged the ordinary functions of his office, he had then alfo the fame
earneftnefs of foul, and the fame folicitous
concern for the fuccefs of his miniftry. Thus,
we have remarked that prayers to God for
profpering his labours occupied the thoughts
of his heart when afleep as well as when
awake; fo entirely was his foul engaged in ac-
complifhing the falvation of immortal fpirits.

Having given this account of the life and
doctrine of Columba, we now turn our eye to
the clofe of his long and ufeful life, as we
have it in the relation of Adomnan [7].

He had fome time ago told that the prayers
of the churches had added four years to the
appointed number of his days. During the
laft of thefe years he alfo dropped feveral hints
to his monks of his being to die in the courfe
of it, that he might thence take occafion to
furnifh them with proper confolation, and for-

---

[7] Ad. iii, 23.

tify and. prepare them againft that mournful
event. One day particularly, (in the month of
May), being unable to walk as far as the weft
end of the ifland, where the monks were at
work, he went thither in a little car, or carriage, as he told, for the laft time ; expreffed
his fatisfaction that his death, which was now
near, had not interfered with the Pafchal folemnity, and damped their feftivity ; and feeing them greatly affected with this hint of his
near departure, he gave them all the confolation in his power before he left them. After
this, having all the ifland before him to the
eaft, he folemnly implored the bleffing of God
upon the ground, and upon all its inhabitants;
adding, that it would go well with them while
they feared God [s].

On the enfuing Sabbath, while, according to
his cuftom on the Lord's day, he was celebrating the folemnity of mafs, his countenance on
a fudden was obferved to glow and colour,
and to give fymptoms of fome unufual and

---

[s] It was on this occafion that Columba prayed (as St.
Patrick is faid to have done in regard to Ireland) that, while
the people of Iona feared God, there fhould not be from that
day forward any ferpent or venomous creature in the ifland
to hurt man or beaft. Ad. ii. 28. " Ex qua die, viperarum
venena trifulcarum linguarum, ufque in hodiernum diem, nullo
modo aut homini aut pecori nocere potuere." Id. iii. 23.

ecſtatic, joy which he then felt: concerning
which he afterwards told ſome of thoſe preſent,
when they aſked the cauſe, that he had ſeen
the Angel of the Lord come to bring to God
ſome depoſit precious in his ſight; but did not
mention particularly what it was.

In eight days after this, in the courſe of the
Sabbath, he went out along with his ſervant
Dermit, and entering the barn, where he ſaw
two heaps of corn, he expreſſed great ſatisfac-
tion, and thanked God, whoſe bounty had thus
provided a ſufficiency of bread for his dear
monks on this year on which he was to leave
them. During this year, ſaid Dermit, wiping
his eyes, you have often made us all ſad by
the mention of your death.—Yes, Dermit, replied the ſaint, but I will now be more explicit
with you, on condition that you promiſe to
keep what I tell you a ſecret till I die; that
there may be no buſtle on that occaſion about
me. Dermit promiſed to do ſo, and thus the
ſaint went on: " This day, in the ſacred vo-
lume, is called the Sabbath, that is, *reſt*, and
will be indeed a Sabbath to me; for it is to
me the laſt day of this toilſome life; the day
on which I am to reſt from all my labour and
trouble: for, on this ſacred night of the Lord,
at the midnight hour, I go the way of my
fathers. So my gracious Lord hath vouchſafed

to intimate ; and all my defire and joy is to be
with him."

Dermit wept bitterly, and the faint adminiftered to him all the confolation in his
power.

After a little time, Dermit being fomewhat
compofed, they left the barn ; and, the faint
refting a little on the way, that tender incident
occured which has been already mentioned [9].
He afterwards afcended a little eminence above
his monaftery, where he ftood, and lifting both
his hands to heaven, prayed God to blefs it
and to make it profper. From thence he returned to his clofet, and having fpent part
of his time there in tranfcribing the Pfalter,
came to that paffage in the 34th Pfalm where
it is faid, *They that feek the Lord fhall not want
any good thing*, he faid, Here I have come to
the end of a page, and to a very proper part for
me to ftop at ; for the following words *(Come,
ye children, hearken unto me ; I will teach you the
fear of the Lord)* will better fuit my fucceffor
than me. I will therefore leave it to Baithen
to tranfcribe them.—He then rofe, and went
to evening fervice in the church, and after
coming home, fat down on his bed, and gave it
in charge to Dermit to deliver the following

<hr />

[9] P. 103.

words to his difciples, as his laft.—" My dying charge to you, my dear children, is, that you live in peace, and fincerely love one another. And if you do this, as becometh faints, the God who comforts and upholds the good will help you: and I, now that I am going to dwell with him, will requeft that you may have both a fufficient fupply of the neceffaries of the prefent tranfitory life, and a fhare in that everlafting blifs which he has prepared for thofe who obferve his holy laws."

After this he refted or remained filent, till the bell was rung for vigils at midnight[1]; when, haftily rifing, and going to church, he arrived there before any other, and kneeled down at the altar to pray. When Dermit, who did not walk or rather run fo hard, approached the church, he perceived it (as did alfo thofe who followed him) all illumined, and, as it were, filled with a heavenly glory, or angelic light[2], which, on his entering the door,

---

[1] To pray at midnight was the general practice of Chriftians in the early ages of the church.

[2] Adomnan gives a beautiful and claffical defcription of two other extraordinary vifions, which, he fays, had been feen on the night on which Columba died (or perhaps of this fame vifion, feen by different perfons and in different places); one of them by a holy man in Ireland (*Lugud Mac-Talcain*), who had told next morning that Columba was dead;

R

immediately vanifhed. Upon which Dermit cried, with a lamentable voice, O my father, where art thou! My father, where art thou!

and the other by a number of fifhermen who had been, that night fifhing in Glen *Fende*, from fome of whom Adomnan had the relation when a boy. The purport of both is, that on the night and hour on which Columba, "the pillar of fo many churches," had departed, a pillar of fire, which illumined the fky, with a light brighter than that of the midday fun, was feen to arife from Iona, while loud and fweet-founding anthems of innumerable choirs of angels afcending with his foul were diftinctly heard; and that when this column reached the heavens, the darknefs again returned, as if the fun had fuddenly fet at noon.—Such lively pictures of the opinions of former times will not difpleafe the antiquary, nor appear infignificant to the good and pious man. The cold fceptic may perhaps fmile at the credulity of former ages: but credulity is more favourable to the happinefs of man, and to the interefts of fociety, than fcepticifm. In the hiftory of all ages and nations, we read of fome fuch extraordinary appearances in certain ftages of fociety. Shall we then refufe all credit to human teftimony; or fhall we allow that a kind Providence may have adapted itfelf to the dark ftate of fociety, and given fuch vifible and ftriking proofs of the connection and communication between this world and a world of fpirits, as may be properly withheld from more enlightened times; which may lefs need them, and perhaps lefs deferve them?

Adomnan fays, that even in his time, a heavenly light and manifeftation of angels was frequently feen at Columba's tomb. "Locum in quo ipfius Sancti paufant offa, ufque hodie eadem cœleftis claritas frequentare non ceffat; et fanctorum frequens vifitatio angelorum."

and groping, without waiting for the lamps, found the faint lying before the altar, in a praying pofture. Dermit, attempting to raife him up a little, fat befide him, fupporting the faint's head upon his bofom till the lights came in, when the brethren, feeing their father dying, raifed all at once a moft doleful cry. Upon this the faint, whofe foul had not yet departed, lifted up his eyes, and (as I was told, fays Adomnan, by thofe who were prefent) looked around him with inexpreffible cheer-fulnefs and joy of countenance; feeing, no doubt, the holy angels who were come to meet his fpirit. He then attempted, with Dermit's affiftance, to raife his right hand to blefs the monks who were about him; and his voice having failed, he made, with his hand alone, the motion which he ufed in giving his bene-diction: after which he immediately breathed out his fpirit; but ftill retained the tranquil fmile, the brightnefs, and the frefh look of his countenance, fo that he had the appearance not of one who was dead, but only fleeping [3].

[3] " After the fpirit had departed, continues Adomnan, when the morning hymns were ended, the facred body was carried from the church to the houfe by the brethren, amidft the loud finging of pfalms, and kept for three days and three nights, which were fpent in the fweet praifes of God. The

Thus, on the 9th day of June 597, and in the 77th year of his age, died Columba; a man, whofe extraordinary piety, parts, and ufefulnefs, accompanied with a perpetual ferenity of mind, cheerfulnefs of countenance, fimplicity of manners, benevolence of heart, and fweetnefs of difpofition, have defervedly raifed to the firft rank of faints or holy men. The contemplation of his life and character may teach all, in every fituation, and efpecially thofe in the facred office, this ufeful and important leffon, That we have in us a capacity, if exerted, of attaining, by the grace of God, to fuch meafures both of holinefs and ufefulnefs, as we are little aware of, unlefs we make a fair trial. And without fuch a trial, it is to

venerable body of our holy and bleffed patron, wrapped in fair linen fheets, and put in a coffin prepared for it, was then buried with all due refpect, to rife in lumiuous and eternal glory on the day of the refurrection."

" Such, was the clofe of our venerable patron's life, who is now, according to the Scriptures, affociated to Patriarchs, Prophets, and Apoftles, and to thofe thoufands of faints who are clothed in white robes, wafhed in the blood of the LAMB, and who follow him whitherfoever he goeth.—Such was the grace vouchfafed to his pure and fpotlefs foul by Jefus Chrift our Lord; to whom, with the Father and the Holy Spirit, be honour and power, and praife, and glory, and eternal dominion, for ever and ever. Amen!"

3

no purpofe that we fee in the lives of holy men how good we may *be* ourfelves, and what good we may *do* to others. Thefe two points are the fum of all that has been advanced in the account which we have given of the life of Columba.

ERRATA.

P. 9, note, *for* " Traide" *read* Triade."

P. 23, l. 4. *for* " Scottifh throne" *read* " Dalriadic province" (in Ulfter).——*Note,* The decifion on this point (alluded to in p. 64) was, that this province belonged to the king of the Scots, by right of inheritance, but that he fhould pay tribute for it to the king of Ireland. A remiffion of the tribute paid by the Scottifh king was obtained by Columba, *Stver. Ketin. ap. Colgan. p.* 115.

P. 83, note, *for* " throne" *read* " Dalriada."

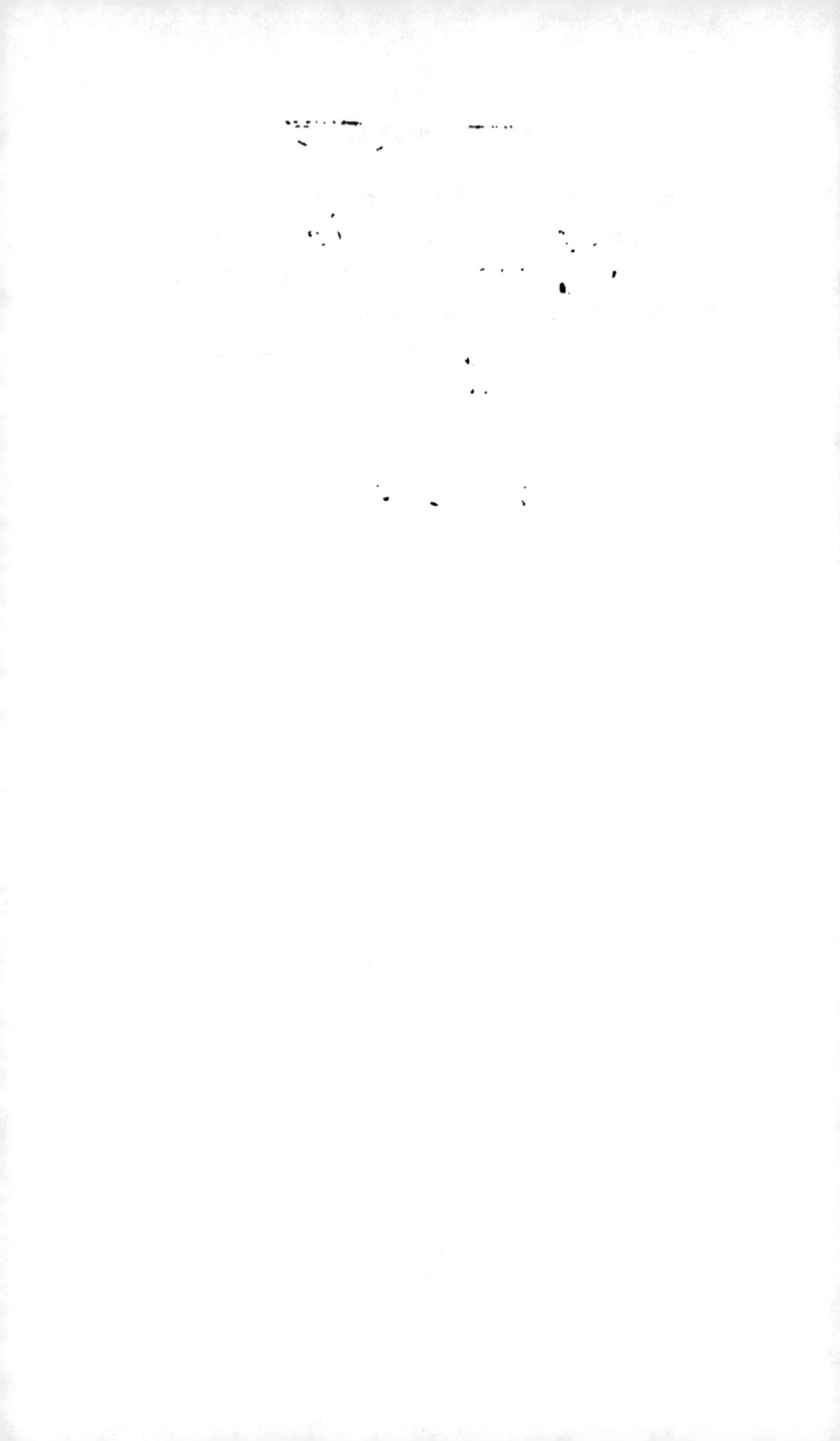

APPENDIX.

After Columba's death, an account of his life was written by many of his friends and disciples. Nine of these are enumerated by Dempster, and the list is increased to fifteen by Colgan. None of their writings are now extant, except those of Cumin and Adomnan. But five or six more of them are frequently quoted by Magnus Odonellus (a prince or nobleman of Tirconnel), who, in the year 1520, compiled a long account of the life of St. Columba, from such monuments as were then extant. This account, which was written in the Irish language, was afterwards abridged, and translated into Latin, by J. Colgan, an Irish friar, who published it in 1647 in his *Trias Thaumaturga*, where it ranks as the *Vita 5ta S. Columbæ.*

Of Columba's own writings, of which Odonellus says there were "a great many, full of piety and devotion, some in "prose, but mostly in Latin or Irish verse," there are now but very few remaining. St. Evin, who wrote a life of St. Patrick in the sixth century, mentions Columba as having wrote a life of that saint (*Vita Tripart. S. Pat.* i. 69). Wilifred (*Ap. Bed.* iii. 25.), the author of the life of St. Ciaran (of Clon. c. 26.), and Alcuin, mention his having composed a monastic *Rule*, which Ware (*de Script. Hib.* i. 2.) says was extant in his time. He also composed a *Rule* for hermits (or *difairt.*), of which Colgan says he had a copy in his possession. He also wrote a number of hymns and poems, both in Irish and Latin, as already mentioned. Ten of the Irish poems were in the poffeffion of Colgan, who (in his *Trias* p. 472.) gives the title and firſt line of each of them. Of theſe, which are probably ſtill extant in Ireland, I have ſeen none but his Farewell to the Monaftery of Durrough.

Of Columba's Latin hymns or poems, Colgan has publiſhed three. One of them was compoſed during a thunder ſtorm in Durrough, or Daire-chalguich ; another of them on the creation, fall of angels, and final judgment, &c. ; and the third, addreffed to the Redeemer, was compoſed, it is ſaid, in conſequence of an obſervation made to him that the Redeemer ought to have been more celebrated in the preceding hymn.

As Columba intended that his diſciples ſhould commit theſe hymns to memory, they are compoſed in a fort of rhyme, agreeably to the form and meaſure of Iriſh poetry, to which they were fo much accuſtomed. From this circumſtance, the ſpecimens of them, given in the notes, may appear ſomewhat ſingular to the Latin reader, who is unacquainted with the rules of Iriſh poetry. To the Engliſh reader the following tranſlations will ſhow the nature of the originals.

HYMN I.

Compofed during a Thunder Storm about the year 550.

GRACIOUS FATHER! bow thine ear *,
And our requeſt in mercy hear:

---

* Noli Pater indulgere
  Tonitrua cum fulgure,
  Ne frangamur formidine
  Hujus atque uredine.

  Te timemus terribilem,
  Nullum credentes fimilem :
  Te cuncta canunt carmina
  Angelorum per agmina :
  Teque exaltant culmina
  Cœli vagi per flamina, &c.

O bid the thunder ceafe to roar,
And let the lightning flafh no more;
Left long in terror we remain,
Or by its ftroke we fhould be flain.

The pow'r fupreme to thee belongs,
Archangels laud thee in their fongs;
The wide expanfe of heav'n above
Refounds thy glory and thy love.

O Saviour of the human race!
Whofe pow'r is equal to thy grace;
For ever be thy name ador'd,
As King fupreme, and only Lord!
To all thy people thou art nigh,
And oft thy grace prevents their cry;
While in the womb the Baptift lay,
(The harbinger to pave thy way),
His foul with grace was amply ftor'd,
To fit him to proclaim his Lord.
—May love and zeal to thee, my God!
Have in my heart a firm abode:
O that the cafket may be fuch
As fits a gem fo very rich!

HYMN II.

On the Creation, Fall of Angels, Final Judgment, &c.

THE God omnipotent, who made the world *,
Is fubject to no change. He was, he is,
And he fhall be: th' ETERNAL is his name.

---

* Altus profator, vetuftus
  Dierum, et ingenitus,
  Erat abfque origine,
  Primordio et crepidine,

S

Equal in godhead and eternal pow'r,
Is Chrift the Son.   So is the Holy Ghoft.
Thefe facred glorious three are but the fame;
In perfons diff'rent, but one God and Lord.

This God created all the heav'nly hofts;
Archangels, angels, potentates and pow'rs;
That fo the emanations of his love
Might flow to myriads, diffufing good.

But from this eminence of glory fell
Th' apoftate Lucifer, elate with pride
Of his high ftation and his glorious form.
Fill'd with like pride, and envy'ng God himfelf
His glory, other angels fhar'd his fate,
While the remainder kept their happy ftate.

'Thus fell a third of the bright heav'nly ftars,
Involv'd in the old ferpent's guilt and fate,
And with him fuffer in th' infernal gulf
The lofs of heav'n, in chains of darknefs bound.

God then to being call'd this lower world,
According to the plan form'd in his mind.
He made the firmament, the earth, and fea,
The fun, the moon and ftars; a glorious hoft!
The earth he clad with herbs for food, and trees,
And then to ev'ry living thing gave birth,
And laft to man, whom he made lord of all.

Eft, et erit in fecula
Seculorum infinita:
Cui eft unigenitus
Chriftus, et Sanctus Spiritus
Coæternus in gloria
Deitatis perpetua, &c.

When angels (the firſt morning ſtars) beheld
The wondrous fabric, with glad ſongs they hymn'd
The praiſe of the Almighty architect,
For ſuch diſplays of wiſdom, pow'r, and love.

But our firſt parents, from their happy ſtate
Seduc'd by Satan, were with terror fill'd,
With dreadful ſights appall'd, till God with grace
Conſol'd their hearts, and Satan's pow'r reſtrain'd.
His providential care he alſo ſhow'd,
And bade the humid clouds diſtil their rains,
And times and ſeaſons in their order run.
Rivers and ſeas (like giants bound in chains)
He forc'd to keep within the limits fix'd,
And flow for ever for the uſe of man.

Lo! earth's vaſt globe, ſuſpended by his pow'r,
On nothing hangs, as on a ſolid baſe.
Hell, too, his word obeys; where monſters dire,
And flames, and fire, and ſmoke, and gnawing worms,
Torment his foes, who gnaſh their teeth with pain.
Though once they ſlighted, now they feel his pow'r,
And muſt reluctantly his will obey.

O happy they who love his holy law,
And in the bleſſings of the ſaints partake!
Who in the paradiſe of God above
Drink of the living ſtream, and eat the fruit
Of that life-giving tree, ordain'd by God
To heal the nations, and to feed the ſoul.

Thrice happy is the ſoul that ſhall aſcend
To this abode of God, when the laſt trump
Shall ſound, and ſhake the earth more than of old,
When Sinai ſhook, and Moſes was afraid.

S ij

This awful day of God the Lord draws nigh,
When earthly objects shall have loft their charm,
And joy or terror fill each human foul.
Then shall we stand before the judgment feat,
To render an account of all our deeds:
Then shall our fins before our face be set,
The books be open'd, and the confcience heard.
None shall be miffing; for the dead shall hear
The voice of God, and from their graves come forth
To join their fouls, and stand before the bar.

Time runs his courfe no more: the wand'ring orbs
Through heaven lofe their courfe: the fun grows dark,
Eclipfed by the glory of the Judge.
The ftars drop down, as, in a tempeft, fruit
Is fhaken from the tree: and all the earth,
Like one vaft furnace, is involv'd in flames.
See! the angelic hofts attend the Judge,
And on ten thoufand harps his praifes hymn.
Their crowns they caft before his feet, and fing,
" Worthy the Lamb that died to be the Judge!
" To Father, Son, and Holy Ghoft, be praife!"

The fentence paft, confuming fire shall feize
The unbelieving, difobedient crowd:
But we who have believ'd, and kept his word,
Shall enter into glory with the Lord;
And there, in diff'rent ranks, we shall receive,
Through grace, rewards proportion'd to our deeds,
And dwell in endlefs glory with our Lord.

Almighty Father, Son, and Holy Ghoft,
Thou ONE Eternal, ever-bleffed God!
To me, the leaft of faints, vouchfafe thy grace!
O may I join the thoufands round thy throne!

HYMN III.

To the REDEEMER.

1. JESUS! may all who trust in thee *
Experience thy love :
That thou art God for evermore
By their salvation prove.

2. In time of trouble and distress
Be thou their faithful friend ;
In all their sorrows comfort them,
And ready succour send.

3. Thou art the Father of the just,
Their souls have life in thee ;
Thou art their God omnipotent,
And evermore shalt be.

4. The world, with all that it contains,
From thee its being had ;
O'er all the nations thou wilt rule,
And judge the quick and dead.

---

* In te Christe credentium
Misereris omnium :
Tu es Deus in secula
Seculorum in gloria.

Deus in adjutorium
Intende laborantium :
Ad dolorum remedium
Festina in auxilium, &c.

5. Thy glory fhines above the fkies,
   Where thou art God and King ;
   And to the New Jerufalem
   Thy people thou wilt bring.

6. Eternal God! who can conceive
   Thy power or thy grace ?
   Through endlefs ages they endure,
   And fill the bounds of fpace.

7. The Father, Son, and Holy Ghoft,
   While I have life I'll praife ;
   And after death, in other worlds,
   The fong again I'll raife.

8. Gracious Saviour of the world !
   The pure are thy delight :
   O give me wifdom from above
   To guide me in the right.

9. Defend me by thy mighty pow'r,
   Until my warfare's o'er,
   And with the martyrs afterwards
   May I thy name adore.

10. As thou didft fuffer on the crofs
    To fave a guilty race,
    Show me thy power, with thy love,
    And glory grant, with grace.

11. Eternal praife to the Moft High,
    The Father and the Son,
    And to the Spirit of all grace,
    Th' eternal Holy One.

12. Protect us, O thou God most high,
Until we reach the place
Where endless anthems we shall sing
Around thy throne of grace.

Another poem or epistle, against avarice, in appropriate
Latin verse, is preferved by *Canifius*, who is difpofed to
afcribe it to the other St. Columba or Columbanus, the
countryman and contemporary of this. It is not unworthy
of either, and may be read as one of the monuments of the
learning of the times, without determining to which of the
two it belongs. The following verfion will give an idea of
it to the Englifh reader, and the original is given in a
note.

EPISTLE to HUNALD. Against Avarice.*

HUNALD! the counfel of Columba hear,
And to thy friend give now a willing ear;

---

* S. COLUMBANI ABBATIS EPISTOLA, in qua detefatur avaritiam, HUNALDO difcipulo.

Sufcipe Hunalde libens, et perlege mente ferena.
Dicta Columbani, fida te voce monentis:
Quæ licet ornatu careant fermonis honefti,
Vota tamen mentifque piæ teftantur amorem.

Vive Deo fidens, Chrifti præcepta fequendo,
Dum modo vita manet, dum tempora certa falutis;
Tempus et illa volat, monentis labitur ætas.
Defpice, quæ pereunt, fugitivæ gaudia vitæ:
Non fragiles fecteris opes et inania lucra,
Nec te follicitet circumflua copia rerum.
Sint tibi divitiæ divinæ dogmata legis,

No ftudied ornament fhall gild my fpeech,
What love fhall dictate, I will plainly preach.

Sanctorumque patrum castæ moderamina vitæ,
Omnia quæ dociles fcripferunt ante magiftri,
Vel quæ doctiloqui cecinerunt carmina vates:
Has cape divitias : femper contemne caducas :
In mentemque tibi veniat tremebunda fenectus,
Quam gelidæ tandem fequitur violentia mortis.
Ultima jam fapiens meditatur tempora vitæ,
Torpentes fenio vires morbofque frequentes,
Incertumque diem lethi certofque dolores.
Multa fenem fragilis vexant incommoda carnis:
Nam macie turpi tabefcunt languida membra,
Tunc genuum junctura riget, venafque per omnes
Illius in toto frigefcit corpore fanguis.
Sic baculo nitens artus fuftentat inertes.
Quid triftes memorem gemitus, quid tædia mentis?
Somnus abeft oculis, illum fonus excitat omnis.
Quid tunc argenti, fulvi quid proderit auri
Improba congeries, multos collecta per annos?
Munera quid procerum? ditis quid prandia'menfæ?
Quid meminiffe juvat tranfactæ gaudia vitæ,
Venerit extremi tandem cum terminus ævi?
Hæc, dum vita volat, vigili qui mente retractat,
Spernit avaritiam, vanofque refutat honores.
Quid modo terrenis mentis intendere curis
Mortales cupiunt? quid turpia lucra fequuntur?
Semper avarus eget, nec habet quod habere videtur.
Ille domi folus nummos abfcondit in arca,
Divitias cumulans, dum fefe nefcit amare,
Plus amat hæredem, fervat cui cuncta fidelis.

O nimium felix, parcus cui fufficit ufus,
Corporis ut curam moderamine temperet æquo,
Non mifera capitur cæcaque cupidine rerum,
Nec majora cupit, quam quæ natura repofcit ;
Non lucri cupidus nummis marfupia replet,
Nec molles cumulat tinearum ad pabula veftes.

Have faith in God, and his commands obey;
While fleeting life allows you here to stay ;
And know, the end for which this life is giv'n,
Is to prepare the soul for God and heav'n.
Despise the pleasures which will not remain;
Nor set thy heart on momentary gain :
But seek for treasures in the sacred page,
And in the precepts of each faint and sage.
These noble treasures will remain behind
When earthly treasures fly on wings of wind.

Pascere non pingui procurat fruge caballos;
Nec trepido tales doluit sub pectore curas,
Ne subitis pereat collecta pecunia flammis;
Aut fracta nummos rapiat fur improbus arca.

Vivitur argento sibe, jam sine vivitur auro ;
Nudi nascuntur, nudos quos terra receptat.
Divitis nigri referantur limina ditis,
Pauperibusque piis cœlestia regna patescunt.
Temnere divitias monuit Salvator avaros ;
Quisquis amat Christum, sequitur vestigia Christi :
Nam brevis et fragilis moriturae gloria carnis
Quicquid habet, rapidi velox fuga temporis aufert,
Pulchre veridici cecinit vox talis vatis,
Tempora dinumerans ævi vitæque caducæ.
Omnia tempus agit, cum tempore cuncta trahuntur :
Alternant alimenta vices et tempora mutant.
Accipiunt alimenta dies noctesque vicissim ;
Tempora sunt florum, retinet sua tempora messis,
Sic iterum spisso vestitur graminæ campus.
Tempora gaudendi ; sunt tempora certa dolendi :
Tempora sunt vitæ ; sunt tristia tempora mortis.
Omnia dat, tollit, minuitque volatile tempus.
Ver, æstas, autumnus, hiems, redit annus in annum.
Omnia cum redeant, homini sua non redit ætas :
Hanc sapiens omni semper reminiscitur hora,
Atque domum luctus epulis præponit opimis.

T

Think of the time when trembling age fhall come,
And the laft meffenger to call thee home.
'Tis wife to meditate betimes on death,
And that dread moment which will ftop the breath,
On all thé ills which age brings in its train,
Difeafe and weaknefs, languor, grief and pain.
The joints grow ftiff, the blood itfelf runs cold,
Nor can the ftaff its trembling load uphold.
And need I fpeak of groans and pangs of mind,
And fleep difturb'd by every breath of wind?
What then avails the heap of yellow gold,
For years collected, and each day re-told?
Or what avails the table richly ftor'd
To the fick palate of its dying lord?
The finful pleafures which have long fince paft,
Are now like arrows in his heart ftuck faft.

He who reflects that Time, on eagle-wing,
Flies paft, and preys on every earthly thing,
Will fcorn vain honours, avarice defpife,
On nobler purfuits bent, beyond the fkies.

Alas! vain mortals, how mifplac'd your care,
When in this world you feek what is not there?
True lafting happinefs is found above,
And heav'n, not earth, you therefore ought to love.
The rich enjoy not what they feem to have,
But fomething more their fouls inceffant crave.
The ufe of riches feldom do they know;
For heirs they heap them, or they wafte in fhow.

O! happy he, to whofe contented mind
Riches feem ufelefs, but to help mankind;
Who neither fquanders what fhould feed the poor,
Nor fuffers Avarice to lock his ftore.

No moths upon his heaps of garments feed,
Nor ferves his corn to feed the pamper'd fteed.
No cank'ring care fhall take his peace away ;
No thief, nor flame, fhall on his fubftance prey.
His treafure is fecure beyond the fkies,
And there he finds it on the day he dies.

This world we enter'd naked at our birth,
Naked we leave it, and return to earth :
Silver and gold we need not much, nor long,
Since to this world alone fuch things belong.
Life's little fpace requires no ample ftore :
Soon heaven opens to the pious poor ;
While Pluto's realms their dreary gates unfold,
Thofe to admit who fet their fouls on gold.

Our Saviour bids us Avarice avoid,
Nor love thofe things which can't be long enjoy'd.
Short, fays the Pfalmift, are the days of man,
The meafure of his life a narrow fpan.
Time flies away ; and on its rapid wing
We fly along, with ev'ry earthly thing,
Yet Time returns, and crowns the Spring with flow'rs,
Renews the feafons, and repeats the hours.
But life returns not with revolving years,
And man, once gone, on earth no more appears.
Wife then is he who makes it his great care,
In this fhort fpace, for heaven to prepare.

From its connection with the fubject, it may not be improper to add the following tranflation of a hymn ufed in
the Office for the Feftival of St. Columba, and publifhed in
Paris, in the year 1620, from an ancient MS. It was probably compofed by Baithen, or fome other of Columba's
difciples, foon after his death.

T ij

Translation of a Hymn used in the Office for the Festival of St. Columba, on the 9th of June.

With snowy pinions soaring high,
The Dove * ascends beyond the sky;
He scorns the earth, he leaves its clay,
And perches in the realms of day.

There his refulgent colours shine,
Reflecting back the light divine.
But here his tender brood he left,
Of their dear parent now bereft.

Yet, ere he mounted to the skies,
With many prayers, tears and cries,
Their charge he gave to Christ his Lord,
To guide them by his gracious word,
And bring them to the same abode
In which their father lives with God.

O God! who didst our father hear,
Be to his children ever near;
And grace vouchsafe to lead us on,
Until we meet him at thy throne †.

---

* Alluding to his name, which means " a Dove."

† Columba penna nivea, collo resplendens roseo,
Loca petit sidera, clauftro mundi luteo.
  Hic nidum sibi posuit, in petra poenitentiae,
Devotos Christo genuit pulles per verbum gratiae.
  Pro dulci cantu, querulis intendebat gemitibus
Crebros adjungens sedulis fletus orationibus.
  Sit Deo soli gloria, qui nos post cursus stadia,
Columbae per suffragia, ducat ad coeli gaudia.
  Amen!

Officium. S. Columba. Ed. Mesfingham, Paris 1620. ex membran. vet. MS.

Of the MONASTERIES *and* CHURCHES *founded by St.* COLUMBA.

Jocelin *(vit. S. Pat.* c. 89.) fays, that Columkille founded 100 monafteries. Hanmer *(in Chron..,p.* 43. &c.) Ufher, and others, fay the fame. Odonellus (iii. 42.) fays, that of monafteries and churches together he founded 300, partly in Ireland, and partly in Scotland. The following is

A Lift of fome of the principal Monafteries and Churches founded by St. Columba in Ireland (of which the names of the firft Abbots, and fome other particulars, may be found in Colgan, and in the Authors which he cites.)

Mon. of Doire-Chalguich, or Durrough, now Derry.
—— of Darmagh (Roboreti campus. Ad.)
Church of Rath-Reghenden, in the diocefe of Derry.
Mon. of Kill-Aibhne, or Kill-Aibhind.
5 —— of Snamh-Luthuir, in Connaught.
—— of Drim-Tuam, in Tirconnel.
—— of Tir-da-chraobh, *al.* mon. of the two rivers.
—— of Drim-finchoil.
—— of Sean-glean, in Tirconnel.
10 —— of Gartan, in do.
—— of Tulach-Dubhglais, in do.
—— of Kill-mac-nenain, in do.
—— of Cluain, or Cluain-enaich, in the diocefe of Derry.
—— of Rath-bè ; long a bifhop's fee in Tirconnel.
15 —— of Drim-cliabh, in the north of Connaught.
—— of Kenannais, *in Media, olim nobile.*
—— of Clauain-mor-Fernard.
—— of Rechrain, *in orient. parte Bregarum.*
—— of Rechlain. ifland.
20 —— of Surd, *olim nobile.*
—— of Torrachan, an ifland, north of Tirconnel.
—— of Rath, in Tirconnel.
—— of Termonn Cethmanaich, *in Tironia.*
—— of S. Columba's Coffer, *olim ditiffimum,* in Ardia.

25 Mon. of Innis-loch-gamhna, in Connaught.
—— of Eas-mac-neirc, in do.
—— of Imleach-foda, *olim nobile*.
—— of Druim-Choluim-cille, in Tir-oileail.
—— of Kill-mor-Dithreibh, in Connaught.
30 —— of Maoin-Cholum-chille, in Leinster.
—— of S. Columba's Coffer, in Media Orientali. (Often pillaged).
—— of Cnoc-na Maoile, in Connaught.
—— of Kill-chuanna, in do.
—— of All-Farannain, in do.
35 —— of S. Columba's Coffer (Scrinium S. Col.) *in Tironia*.
—— of Kill-lukin, in Connaught.
—— of Cluain-ogcormacain, *in regione Siol-mhuir'ich*.
—— of Kill-tuama, in Tir-maine, Connaught.
—— of Difert-Egnioh, in Innis-owen.
40 —— of Cluain-maine, in do.
Church of Kill-matoige, *diocef. Med*.
Mon. of Fathen-mura, in Innis-owen.
—— of Uifge-chaoin, diocefe of Derry.
—— of Baile-mag-rabhartaich, in do.
45 —— of Teach-Bhaithen, in Tirconnel.
—— of Cluain-laoidh, in do.
—— of Both-medha, in Ulster.
—— of Tamlacht-Fionlugain, diocefe of Derry.
—— of Difert-Hi Thuachuill, in do.
50 —— of Dun-bò, in do.
—— of Aregal, in do.
—— of Gleann-Choluim-chille, in Tuam.
—— of Kill-Cholgain, in Clonfert.
—— of Baile-megrabhartich, in Tir-Aodh, (in which was kept Columba's book, called *Cathach*, from its being carried before the army to the field of battle).
55 —— of Kill-bhairrind, in Tir-Aodh.
—— of Regles Choluim-chille, in Ardmagh.

To thefe, fays Colgan, may be added almoft all the other churches in Tirconnel, many of thofe of Lower Connaught; and all the churches, of which we find his difciples had the charge, as Innis-cail, Innis Mhuiredhich, Port-Lomain, Teach-Earnain, &c.

Of the monafteries and churches founded by St. Columba in Scotland, no particular account can be given, as the records of them have not been preferved. We can only fay in general, that he planted churches in all the Weftern Ifles, and in all the territory of the ancient Scots and northern Picts, and fome even beyond them. Colgan, and authors cited by him, fay he founded the church of Dunkeld, the monaftery of Inch-colm in the Forth, and the monaftery of Govan on the Clyde. Adomnan, befides the chief monaftery of Iona, mentions feveral more in the Weftern Ifles; fuch as that of Achaluing, in Ethica; Himba, or Hinba, and Elen-naomh; alfo Kill-Diun, or Dimha, at Lochava (or Lochow). Moft of our parifhes ftill bear the names of his difciples, and tell their founder; and the vaft number of places, whofe names begin with *Kill*, fhows how thick our churches were anciently planted; fo that there is much reafon to believe that the largeft number afcribed to Columba is not above the mark. Providence fmiled in a remarkable manner on his labours, and his fuccefs was aftonifhing. It is no wonder that fo extraordinary a man fhould have been fo much revered while alive, and his memory fo much refpected after his death. Accordingly, he is ftyled by foreign, as well as by domeftic writers, the Apoftle of the Scots and Picts, the patron Saint of both, and the joint patron of Ireland, " Pictorum et Scotorum Albienfium apoftolus, et utri-" ufque Scotiæ patronus;" *S. Evin. Vit. S. Pat.* " Doc-" tor Scotorum et Pictorum;" *Mat. Weft. ad ann.* 566. *and Sigibert. in Chron.* " S. Columba, abbas Hienfis, Scoto-" rum et Pictorum Doctor et Apoftolus;" *Colgan,* 664.; and though only an abbot, he had the fingular privilege of exercifing (as did his fuccefTors) a jurifdiction over all their bi-

fhops, being primate of all their churches, " Pictorum et
" Scotorum Primas ;" *Colgan.* p. 498. Notkerus Balbulus,
who ranks Columba *almoft* with the firft apoftles, calls him
alfo " Primate of all the Irifh bifhops" (Omnium Hibernienfi-
um-epifcoporum Primas ; *Martyrol.* 9. *Jun.*), which the author
of the life of St. Farran *(Colgan. Trias.* p. 463.) fays he was
made at the great council of Drimkeat. His fucceffors, the
abbots of Iona, feem for a confiderable time to have had the
fame pre-eminence in Ireland as well as in Scotland. The
acts of a fynod of the clergy of Ireland, at which Adomnan
prefided in 695, are called " The Canons of Adomnan." *Col-*
gan. p. 665. ; and in 925 Maolbride feems to have had equal
authority, as may be inferred from the annals of the *Quat.*
Magiftri. ad ann. 925. (See Chron. annexed).

In after times, St. Columba was confidered as the patron
faint of the ancient Scots and Picts ; and the patron faint of
Ireland, in conjunction with St. Patrick and St. Bridget.
" Sunt enim hi tres SS. Patricius, Columba, et Brigida tres
" præcipui et generales univerfæ Hiberniæ patroni;" *Marty-*
rol. Dungallenfe. " Conftat hos tres Sanctos coli olim tanquam
" univerfæ Hiberniæ communes patronos ;" *Colgan.* p. 453.
To this honour, his merit in Ireland, as well as in Scotland,
gave him the ampleft title. " Columba Apoftolus Albaniæ
" præcipuus poft. S. Patricium præco, et feminator religionis
" in univerfa fere Hibernia et Albania;" *Annal. Quat. Mag.*
ad ann. 596.

Both nations held him in fuch reverence, that they thought
their fecurity depended upon their having his remains in their
poffeffion. The Pictifh Chronicle fays, that Kenneth Mac-
Alpin, after his conqueft of the Picts, carried the relics of
Columba to a church which he had built in his new territory,
(A. D. 489.) ; and the Irifh writers relate, that they were
carried to Ireland, and placed in Down, in the fame tomb
with St. Patrick and St. Bridget, (*Martyrol. Dungallenfe*).
Giraldus Cambrenfis fays, they were carried thither in 1185,

z

by order of John de Curci, and repeats the well known
lines,

> Hi tres in Duno, tumulo tumulantur in uno,
> Brigida, Patricius, atque Columba pius.

These opinions and stories may serve to show the veneration
which the people of both nations had for the memory and
remains of Columba.

But the fame of Columba, and the veneration for his
name, extended much farther than Britain. and Ireland. A-
domnan (iii. 23.) observes, that "though Columba lived
"in a small remote island of the British ocean, yet God had
"done him the honour to make his name renowned, not
"only through all Britain and Ireland, but through Spain,
"France, and Italy, and particularly in Rome, the greatest
"city in the world. Thus, adds he, God honoureth those
"who honour him; for which his holy name be praised."

Odonellus, who cites this passage from Adomnan, says, in
still stronger terms, that whilst the saint was yet alive almost
all the countries of Europe sounded with his fame. Several
testimonies of foreign writers have been occasionally produced already to this purpose; to which I shall here add that
of Anthony Yepez, who (in Chron. General. Ordin. S. Be-
ned.) says, ad ann. 565. Sub idem tempus, &c. " About this
"time flourished the two Irish saints, of the name of Co-
"lumbanus, or Columba; both of whom were so illustrious,
"that either of them would be alone sufficient to give cele-
"brity to the whole nation to which they belonged. As
"they had the same name, so they had also the same gene-
"rous zeal, and made the same noble exertions to spread the
"gospel among heathen nations in foreign lands.".

U

Of, the DISCIPLES of St. COLUMBA.

To the great fuccefs of Columba, the inftruments employed under him muft have contributed not a little. His difciples were men of learning, as well as of zeal and piety.
He chofe men of this ftamp for his firft affociates; and his
own feminaries furnifhed him afterwards with a fufficient fupply of the fame kind. Learning, when he fet out in life,
was in a very flourifhing ftate in Ireland. In many of the
lives of the Irifh faints, written in that age, we read of numerous fchools, well attended, and taught by learned and
aged mafters; which could not have been the cafe, if, as
fome maintain, letters had been introduced into the country
no fooner than the time of St. Patrick. So general a dif-
fufion of learning, and fuch acquaintance with the learned
languages as Columba's mafters and his contemporaries poffeffed, could not poffibly have taken place in fo fhort a period. But without entering further into this fubject at prefent, it is enough to fay, that Columba found and chofe men
of learning, as well as of zeal and piety, to fuperintend his
feminaries, and to conduct his miffions; while he himfelf,
with unwearied diligence, went through occafionally from
province to province, through the whole of his immenfe
diocefe *.

We had occafion to obferve before, that he was at great
pains to felect the moft promifing youths, and the children
of pious parents, for his difciples, and that the courfe of

---

* Delata cænobii adminiftratione cuidam e fua familia probo Seniori,
omnes ipfe regni provincias continuo peragrans, urbes, oppida, pagos
circuiens, colendis populorum moribus totus incumbebat: paffim tem-
pla, paffim monafteria extruere, ac dignis facrorum adminiftris pro-
videre.

                                        - *Odonell.* i. 58.

education and probation prefcribed by him was very long ; fo
that the learning, as well as the piety and prudence of every
candidate, was well proved before he was intrufted with the
cure of fouls. We have feen a man, who thought himfelf already qualified for entering into orders, obliged by Columba
to fpend no lefs than feven years more in education and preparation before he could be ordained to the facred office.
Sanctity and zeal, when thus accompanied with learning,
could not fail to make the difciples of Columba both refpected
and ufeful.

The inftituting of fchools and feminaries of learning, in
which men were thus prepared for the miniftry, and trained
up from their infancy in the acts and habits of their office,
and kept till their character was fully formed, and their qualifications well known and proved, had a powerful tendency
to make their future labours fuccefsful. From his firft rho-
nafteries in Ireland, Columba drew the neceffary fupplies, till
that over which he himfelf prefided in Iona was in condition
to furnifh as many as he needed. The excellency of his plan
was fufficiently proved by the effect which it produced.

Another circumftance which greatly contributed to the
fuccefs of Columba, efpecially in Ireland, was the high rank
of many of his difciples. A great number of them were,
like himfelf, of the family of Conal Gulbann, fon of Niall
Naoighealbach (or " Neil of the Nine Hoftages"), monarch
of Ireland. That country, long haraffed by civil wars, liftened
gladly to a fyftem which propofed *peace on earth ;* and which
its effect, upon thofe who firft profeffed it, fhowed to be fully
adequate to all that it propofed. Hence, many of the nobility not only embraced but preached the gofpel, and ranked
themfelves among the followers and difciples of Columba.
It was then the fafhion among great men to be great faints ;
a fafhion which is long of coming round again, although one
fhould think that felf-prefervation might now give the alarm,
and help to bring it about.

U ij

Among the circumstances which conduced to Columba's success, may be mentioned the unusual length to which the lives of many holy men, who then preached the gospel, were preserved. Their extreme temperance, constant exercise, and inward joy and serenity of mind, would no doubt contribute to health and long life. But that the duration of it, accompanied with health and usefulness, should have been so long as we find from a variety of concurring testimonies it often was, can be ascribed only to the kind and particular providence of God being peculiarly concerned about their preservation. The age of St. Patrick, and some more, may probably be exaggerated. But it is pleasing to find the oldest of them (what is more credible than his age) represented as active and cheerful to the last, after all the toil of his daily duty.

> Tri fiched bliadhan fa thri
> Soeghal an chredhuil Chrumanl,
> Gan tamh, gan ghalar, sofdach
> Iar maifreann iar ceolabhradh.   *Colgan, 175.*

Of Columba's own scholars or disciples above one hundred had the honour of being fainted, and their festivals observed by the gratitude of those places which they benefited by their labours, as we find from the accounts given of them by various authors. The following is

A List of some of the most eminent of COLUMBA's immediate Disciples and Contemporaries.

(The Twelve who came with Columba at first to Iona are marked thus *).

St. Aidan, or Aodhan, fon of Libher; afterwards bp. of Lindisfarn. *Bed.* l. iii.
St. Aidan, fon of Kein, abbot of Cuil-uisc. (There are twenty-seven faints of this name).

St. Ailbhe, fon of Ronan.

St. Aonghus, of Dermagh.

5 St. Baithan, of Doire-chalguich.

St. Baithen, fon of Brendan, ab. of Hi.

St. Barrind, ab. of Kill-barrind.

St. Becan, fon of Ernan, brother of Cumin Fionn.

St. Bec, or Beg-bhile, fon of Tighearnach.

10 St. Berach, a monk of Hi; abbot of Cluain-choirpe.

St. Berchan, or Barchan. *Ad.* iii. 21.

St. Bran, or Branni', in Doire-chalguich, nephew of Columba.

St. Cailten, of Kill-Diun or Dimha, at Loch-ava.

*St. Carnan, fon of Brandubh.

15*St. Ceata, or Catan; fuppofed by fome to be the bp. Ceadan of *Bede;* by others the Cetheus, furnamed Peregrinus, faid by *Herman. Greven.* to have fuffered martyrdom in Italy.

St. Ceallach, bp. of the Mercians, in England.

St. Cobhran, fon of Enan, nephew of Columba.

*St. Cobhthach, fon of Brendan, and brother of St. Baithen.

St. Colgu, or Colgan, of Kill-cholgan, in Connaught.

20 St. Colgan, fon of Aodh Draighneach, a monk of Hi.

St. Collan, of Dermagh.

St Colman, or Columan, founder of the mon. of Snamh-luthir.

St. Colman, ab. of Hi, and afterwards of Lindiafarn.

St. Colman, fon of Comhgell; who died in 620.

25 St. Colman, abbot of Rechrain.

St. Colman, fon of Enan.

St. Colman, fon of Tighearnach, brother to Beg-bhile Connan and Cuan.

St. Colman, fon of Ronan.

St. Colum Crag, of Enach in Ulfter.

30 St. Coman, or Comhan, brother to St. Cumin.

St. Comgan (or Caomhghan), fon of Deghille, and fifter's fon of Columba.

St. Conall, ab. of Innis-caoil, in Tirconnel.

St. Conna, or Connan, furnamed Dil, fon of Tighear-nach.

St. Conacht, fon of Maoldraighneach.

35 St. Conrach, Mac-Kein, of Dermagh mon.

St. Conftantin, or Cufandin, king of Cornubia, faid by Fordun to have prefided over the monaftery of Govan, upon Clyde, and to have converted the people of Kintyre, where he fays he fuffered martyrdom.

St. Cormac Hua Liethain, ab. of Darmagh.

St. Corman, faid to have been the firft miffionary to the Northumbrians: Flour. A. D. 630.

St. Cuannan, ab. of Kill-chuannain, in Connaught.

40 St. Cuan, or Coan, fon of Tighearnach.

St. Cuchumin Mac-kein, ab. of Hi.

St. Cumin, furnamed Fionn, or Fair, ab. of Hi, who wrote Columba's life.

St. Dachonna, ab. of Eas-mac-neirc.

St. Dallan Forguill, formerly a bard or poet.

45 St. Dermit, of the defcendants of K. Leogaire.

St. Dima, afterwards a bp. of the Mercians, in England.

*St. Eochadh, or Eochadh Torannan.

St. Enna, fon of Nuadhan, ab. of Imleachfoda, in Connaught.

*St. Ernan, uncle to Columba, and ab. of Himba.

50 St. Ernan, ab. of Drim-tuam, in Tirconnel.

St. Ernan, ab. of Torrachan; of the race of K. Niall.

St. Ernan, of Teach-Ernain.

B. Eoghan, or Eoghanan, a Pictifh prefbyter.

St. Failbhe, ab. of Hi.

55 St. Farannan, ab. of All-Farrannain, in Connaught.

St. Fiachna, of Acha-luing, Ethica.

St. Fechno, fon of Rodan: flour. 580. *Martyr. Anglic.*

St. Fergna (Virgnous), ab. of Hii.

60 St. Finan, furnamed Lobhar ; ab. of Sourd, near Dublin.

St. Finan, or Finthan, ab. of Rath, in Tirconnel.

St. Finan, or Feimin, ab. of Magh-chofgain.

St. Finan, an anchorite ; fuppofed by fome to be the fame with the preceding.

St. Finan, who fucceeded Aidan as bp. of Lindisfarn.

65 St. Finbarr, ab. of Drim-choluim, in Connaught.

St. Finnchan, ab. of Ardchaoin.

St. Finnlugan, a monk of Hi.

St. Finten, fon of Aodh, founder of the mon. of Caille-Abhind.

B. Genere, or Gueren, a Saxon, or Anglo-Saxon.

70*St. Grellan, fon of Rodan, or Grellan Aoibhleach.

St. Hilary, or Elaire, fon of Fintan, and brother of St. Aidan.

St. Lafran, fon of Feradach ; ab. of Darmagh.

St. Lafran, called Hortulanus, or Gardener.

St. Lafran, fon of Deghille, and brother of St. Bran.

75 St. Lafran, or Lafar, fon of Ronan.

St. Libhran, from Connaught.

St. Loman, of Lochuair.

St. Luga Ceanaladh, a monk of Hi.

*St. Lugaide, of Cluain-laogh.

80 St. Lugaid, ab. of Cluain-finchoil.

St. Lugaid, furnamed Laidir, of Tir-da-chraobh.

St. Lugbe Mac-cumin, a monk of Hi, ab. of Elen-nao'.

St. Lugbe Mac-Blai', a monk of Hi.

St. Lughne Mac-cumin, brother of St. Lugbe.

85 St. Lughne Mac-Blai', brother of Lugbe Mac-Blai'.

St. Mernoc, or Marnoc, of Cluain-reilgeach.

St. Miril, fifter's fon of Columba.

St. Maolchus, brother to St. Mernoc.

St. Maoldubh, of Cluin-chonair.

90 St. Maoldubh, fon of Enan.

St. Moab, or Abban, his brother.

B. Maolcomha, fon of Aodh Mac-Aimirich, from a king
became a monk.

S. Maol-Odhrain, a monk of Hi.

B. Maol-umha, fon of Beothan, king of Ireland, a monk
of Hi.

95 St. Mochonna, fon of Fiachna, king of Ulfter, afterwards a Piſtiſh biſhop.

*St. Mac-cuthen, faid by Uſher to have wrote a life of
St. Patrick.

St. Moluan, a monk of Hi.

St. Moluoc, of the race of Conal Gulbann, bp. of Lif-
more, died in 588.

St. Mothorian, ab. of Drim-cliabh.

100 St. Munna, fon of Tulchan, ab. of Teach-mhunna.

St. Pilo, an Anglo-Saxon, a monk of Hi.

*St. Odhran, who died foon after he came to Hi, 27th
October.

St. Offin, or Offian, ab. of Cluain-mor. There were feveral faints of this name. A poetical dialogue between one of this name and St. Patrick is ſtill repeated, which Colgan (p. 215.) obferves could not have
been compofed by the fon of Fingal, who lived long
before.

*St. Rus, or Ruffen, ſtyled by Maguir " de infulis Pic-
torum."

105*St. Scandal, fon of Brefal, ab. of Kill-chobhrain.

St. Segin, fon of Fiachri, ab. of Hi.

St. Segen, fon of Ronan, ab. of Bangor in 664.

St. Senach, half-brother of Columba, ab. of Doire-brof-
gaidh.

St. Senan, a monk of Darmagh.

110 St. Sillean, fon of Neman, a monk of Hi.

St. Suibhne, fon of Curtre, ab. of Hi.

St. Ternoc, of Ari-molt, near Loch-Ern, in Ulfter.

*St. Torannan, afterwards ab. of Bangor, as Colgan
thinks.

2

St. Trenan Mac-Rintir, a monk of Hi.

115. B. Tulchan, father of St. Munna, &c. who followed his
sons to Hi.

Such as wish to know more of these faints, and others, may
consult Colgan, Cathald, Maguir, Gorman, the Martyrologies
of Dungallan, Tamlact, &c. &c. with the authors cited by
them.

A brief Account of Iona, and of Columba's Succeffors.

Before Columba died, he had got his chief feminary in
Icolumkill or Iona put in such a state, that he was able to
speak with confidence of its future glory and fame. His difciples accordingly supported its credit for many ages, and
supplied not only their own, but other nations, with learned
and pious teachers. "From this neft of Columba, says Odo-
" nellus, these facred doves took their flight to all quarters."
The other Columbanus, who, after spending some time in the
monaftery of Bangor, paffed from thence to France, afterwards to Germany, and at laft to Italy, and "filled all those
" regions with monafteries," (*Ant. Ypez in Chron. General.
ad. ann. 565.*); paved the way for them into all these countries, into which they poured in such numbers, that both Ypez
and St. Bernard (*Vit. Malachie*) compare them to hives of
bees, or to a spreading flood. Wherever they went they dif-
feminated learning and true religion, of both which they feem
to have poffeffed the greateft share of any fociety then in
Europe, and feem to have done more than any other towards
the revival of both, when they were at the loweft ebb.

Foreign and Romifh writers, accuftomed to diftinguifh
monks by their different orders, speak of the difciples of Columba in the fame manner, and call them by different names,
such as, "Ordo Apoftolicus," (*Gefner*); "Ordo Divi Co-
" lumbæ," "Congregatio Columbina," (*Colgan*); and "Or-

X

do pulchræ focietatis," *(Ware)* ; but they themfelves feem
to have affumed no other name than that of *Famuli Dei,* or
fervants of God ;" or in their own language *Gille-De,* which
was Latinized into Keledeus, (as Comganus Kele-De, or Keledeus ; Ængufinus Keledeus, &c. *ap. Colgan.*), whence the
Englifh name of *Culdees.* Thefe were generally formed into
focieties, confifting each of twelve and an abbot, after the
example of their mafter, or of Chrift and his apoftles ; and
their foreign miffions were commonly conducted on a fimilar
plan.

    Iona continued to be the *Archicenobium,* or chief mona-
ftery, and its abbots the heads of all monafteries and congre-
gations of the followers of Columba in Scotland and Ireland,
for feveral ages, to which all its bifhops were fubject. The
firft check to its celebrity was the invafion of the Norwegians
and Danes in the beginning of the ninth century. By them
it was repeatedly pillaged and burnt, and its monks and abbots maffacred. ' Soon after, it came to be under their fettled
dominion, together with the reft of the Weftern Ifles. As
thofe barbarians held learning in no eftimation, the college of
Iona, though it continued to exift, began to decline, and had
its connection with Britain and Ireland in a great meafure cut
off. Dunkeld affected then, for fome time, to be the Primate's
feat in Scotland, but did not long maintain its claim ; for
about the end of the 9th, or beginning of the 10th century,
the legend of St. Regulus, and the apparition of St. Andrew,
were invented ; in confequence of which, with the aid of king
Grig, St. Andrew's came to be confidered as the principal fee
of Scotland, and St. Andrew to be confidered as the tutelar
faint inftead of St Columba.

    Still, however, the Culdees, or clergy of the order of Co-
lumba, retained their influence and refpect, and often elect-
ed the bifhops of their bounds. At length, in the 12th and
13th centuries, the Romifh monks poured into the kingdom,
fupplanted the Culdees, and by degrees got poffeffion of all

their monafteries. The followers of Columba, after their great and firft concern of eftablifhing Chriftianity in the kingdom was over, and religion fully fettled, did not think it unlawful to marry (*Keith, Sir J. Dalrymple,* &c.), and to take the charge of families as well as of parifhes. The new monks, on the other hand, lived in celibacy, affected greater purity,[note] and had more ceremony and fhow; fo that the popular tide foon turned in their favour. The Culdees exifted no longer in colleges, but for a long time after they continued to teach true Chriftianity apart; fo that the reign of error in thefe lands was very fhort, and the darknefs of its night was intermixed with the light of many ftars.

From thefe notices of Columba, and of his difciples, we may well apply to him the beginning of his own ode to Ciaran.

> *Quantum, Chrifte! apoftolum*
> *Mundo mififti hominem ?*
> *Lucerna hujus infulæ, &c.*

> A great apoftle fent by God
>   Hath blefs'd this ifle with light;
> His beams, diffus'd through all the land,
>   Difpell'd the gloom of night.

A Chronicle *of fome events connected with the* Monastery *of* Hi, *or* Iona. *From the Annals of Quatuor Mag. Ulfter, Colgan, Ir. Martyrologies,* &c. &c.

A. D.
563. St. Columba arrived in Hi, on Pentecoft eve.
563. St. Odhran dies, 27th of October.
572. Conall king of the Scots, who gave Hi to Columba, died.
574. The great Council of Drimkeat was held.

583. Brude, fon of Maolchan, king of the Picts, died.

597. St. Columba, the apoftle of Albin, died; *ætat.* 77.

600. St. Baithen, fon of Brendan, abbot of Hi, died.

601. St. Laifran, fon of Feradach, ab. of Hi, died.

622. St. Fergna, furnamed the Briton, ab. of Hi, died.

635. St. Aidan, (Mac Libher) and others, fet out for England from Iona, at the defire of king Ofwald, to convert his people to Chriftianity.

651. St. Segin, fon of Fiachri, ab. of Hi, died.

651. St. Aidan, bifhop or abbot of Lindisfarn in England, died. (A number of his fucceffors, as Cellach, Fintan, Dima, Colman, &c. were alfo from Hi.)

654. St. Suibhne, fon of Curtre, ab. of Hi, died.

660. St. Colman became ab. of Hi, but foon after went to be abbot of Lindisfarn, which he refigned in 664, and returned to Hi; after which he went to Ireland, and built the monafteries of Innfe-bofionn and Magheo.

668. St. Cumin (Fionn) ab. of Hi, the biographer of Columba, died.

677. St. Failbhe, ab. of Hi, died.

684. St. Adomnan (or *Adhamhnan*), ab. of Hi, goes to reclaim from the Anglo-Saxons fome captives and plunder; was honourably received, and obtained all he wanted.

686. St. Adomnan, on a fecond embaffy, got 60 captives reftored from the Saxons to Ireland.

695. St. Adomnan holds a Synod in Ireland; the acts of which are called " The Canons of Adomnan."

703. St. Adoman, ab. of Hi, and biographer of Columba, died, *ætat.* 78.

708. St. Conamhal, or Conain, fon of Failbhe, ab. of Hi, died.

710. St. Caide, or Caidan, ab. of Hi, died.

713. St. Dorbhen Fada, ab. of Hi, died.

714. St. Faolchuo, fon of Dorbhen Mac Teinne, made ab. of Hi, *et.* 74.

714. The family of Hi (the monks) expelled beyond Drim-albín, by Nectan king of the Picts.

716. St. Duncha (or Duncan), fon of Cinnfaóla, ab. of Hi, died ; and Faolchuo, who had refigned his office to him, again refumes it.

720. St. Faolchuo, fon of Dorben, ab. of Hi, died ; *Quat. Mag.* The Annals of Ulfter place his death in 723, and call him Faolan ; which is the name retained by fome of our old parifhes.

725. St. Killean, or Cillian, furnamed Fada, ab. of Hi, died.

729. St. Egbert, who had remained 13 years in Hi, died.

744. Many of the people of Hi perifhed in a great ftorm.

747. St. Killean, furnamed Droicheach, ab. of Hi, died. (An. Ult. 751.)

754. St. Failbhe II. ab. of Hi, died, *etat.* 87.

762. St. Slebhen, fon of Conghal, ab. of Hi, died.

765. B. *(Beatus)* Nial, furnamed Frafach, king of Ireland (who had abdicated his kingdom, and had been for eight years in Hi), died.

767. St. Suibhne II. ab. of Hi, died. (An. Ult. fay in 771.)

777. St. Muredhach (or Murdoch), fon of Huagal, prior of Hi (ab.), died.

786. B. Artgal Mac Catheld, king of Connaught, who had abdicated, died in pilgrimage in Hi, in the eighth year of his pilgrimage.

793. Devaftation of all the ifles by foreigners.

797. St. Brefal, fon of Seigen, ab. of Hi (for 30 years), died.

St. Conmhal, ab. of Hi *(fcriba felectiffimus)*, died.

797. Hi burnt by foreign pirates.

801. Hi again burnt by pirates, and many of the family deftroyed in the flames.

805. Of the family of Hi, 68 killed by foreigners.

2

810. St. Kellach, fon of Conghal, ab. of Hi, died.

815. Conftantin (or Cufandin), king of the Picts, builds the church of Dunkeld.

816. S. Dermit, ab. of Hi, goes to Albin with Columba's coffer or box, *(fcrinium)*,

823. St. Blamhac, fon of Flanni, ab. of Hi, crowned with martyrdom, being flain by the Nortmans (Norwegians) and Danes.

827. Unguft II. king of the Picts, founded Kilrimont, (St. Andrew's).

843. Kenneth Mac Alpin, after his conqueft of the Picts, removes from the W. to the E. coaft.

848. Juraftach, ab. of Hi, goes to Ireland with Columkille's facred things.

849. Kenneth (III.) tranfported the relics of Columba to his new church. *Pict. Chron.*

852. Aulay *(Amhlaidh)*, king of Lochlin, came to Ireland, and laid it under tribute.

853. The Coarb * (fucceffor or reprefentative) of Columkille, a wife and excellent man, martyred among the Saxons.

863. St. Cellach, fon of Ailild, ab. of Hi, died in the land of the Cruthens (Picts.)

864. Tuahal, Mac Artgufa, Abp. of Fortren, and abbot of Dun-Caillen (Dunkeld), died.

875. St. Columba's box is carried to Ireland, left it fhould fall into the hands of the Danes.

877. B. Ferach Mac Cormaic, ab. of Hi, died. (Ann. Ult. fay in 879.)

890. St. Andrew's, about this time, made independent on Iona, by King Grig. *Reg. S. And.*

---

* Coarb, or comhfhorb, " a *comb, i. e.* con, and *forb,* ager, patrimoni-
" um. Ufurpatur pro fucceffione in dignitate Ecclefiaftica ;" *Colgan.*
Coàrb, or còirb, is ftill ufed in Gaelic to denote one's equal.

890. St. Flan, or Flanna, fon of Maolduine, ab. of Hi, died : *in pace dormivit.*

925. St. Maolbride, fon of Dornan, Coarb (fucceffor) of SS. Pat. Col. and Adomnan, died : " Caput religi-" onis univerfæ Hiberniæ, et majoris partis Europæ " in venerabili feneftute obiit, 22 Feb." *Quat. Mag.*

935. St. Aonghus, fon of Murchartach, co-adjutor of the ab. of Hi, died.

937. Dubharb, Coarb of Colum-kille and Adomnan, refted in peace.

945. St. Caoinchomrach, ab. of Hi, died.

958. Dubhdhuin, Coarb of Columkill, died.

964. St. Fingin, bp. of Hi, died.

978. St. Mugron, a bp. ; fcribe, and notable teacher, fur-named *Nan-tri-rann,* Coarb of Columkill in Ireland and Scotland, died : *felicem vitam finivit.*

979. Amhlua (or Aulay), fon of Sitric, prince of the Nort-mans (or Danes), after his defeat in the battle of Temora, took refuge in Hi, where he died.

985. The ifland of Hi pillaged on Chriftmas eve by the Nortmans, who killed the abbot and 15 of the learned of the church.

997. Patrick, Coarb of Columkill, died, *et.* 83.

988. Duncha, Coarb of Columkill, died.

1004. B. Maolbrighde Hua Remed, ab. of Hi, died.

1009. Martan Mac Cineadh, Coarb of Columkill, died.

1010. Muredach, Coarb of SS. Columba and Adomnan, an eminent profeffor of theology at Ardmagh, died.

1015. B. Flannai Abhra, ab. of Hi, died.

1057. Robhertach Mac Donell, Coarb of Columkill, died.

1070. B. Macbaithen, ab. of Hi, died.

1093. Magnus, king of Norway, fubjugates the W. ifles.

1099. B. Duncha, fon of Moenach, ab. of Hi, died.

1126. The firſt legate (John of Crema) comes to Scotland ; (which is the firſt trace of Papal power there).

1152. Card. Jo Papiro arrives in Ireland with four ſtoles or robes, ſent by the Pope to four archbiſhops of Ireland.

1185. The relics o S. Columba brought to Down by order of Jo. de Curci, (according to *Gir. Cambrenſis.*)

1178. St. Pàtrician Huabranain, a venerable and holy bp. died in Hi.

1188. B. Amblua Hua Doighre, a pilgrim in Hi, died in a venerable old age.

1199. St. Muireach Hua Baodain died in Hi.

1203. Ceallach built a monaſtery in Hi, in oppoſition to the learned of the place ; upon which the clergy of the north of Ireland held a meeting ; after which they came to Hi, and demoliſhed the monaſtery of Ceallach.

Kings contemporary with St. Columba.

Of the Scots.	Piɛts.	Strathclyde.	Ireland.
Conal I. be-} gan to reign} A.D. 560. Aidan - - 575.	Brude II. 557. Garnat IV. 587.	Morken. Roderk.	Dermit I. 544. Fergus} Donald I.} 565. Amirach 566. Beothan} Eoghan} 569. Ed (or Aodh) I.} 572.

1. C. Cornelii Taciti Opera, recognovit, emendavit, sup-
plementis explevit, Notis, Differtationibus, Tabulis Geogra-
phicis illuftravit, Gabriel Brotier, 4 tom. 4to, 5 l. 10 s.
boards.

2. Idem Liber, 4 tom. royal 8vo, 3 l. 3 s. boards.

    In this edition are included the Notes added by Brotier
    to the Paris 12mo edition, incorporated with thofe he
    had formerly publifhed with the 4to; and it is thus
    rendered more complete than either of the Paris
    editions.

3. Q. Horatii Flacci Opera, cum Scholiis veteribus caftiga-
vit, et Notis illuftravit, Gulielmus Baxterus. Varias Lectiones
et Obfervationes addidit Jo. Matthias Gefnerus. Quibus et fuas
adfperfit Jo. Carolus Zeunius, Prof. Gr. Litt. Viteberg.
Editio nova, priore emendatior, 4to, 1 l. 4 s. boards.

4. Idem Liber, royal 8vo, 12 s. boards.

5. Publii Virgilii Maronis Bucolica, Georgica et Æneis, ad
Optimorum Exemplarium fidem recenfita, poft 12mo, 3 s. 6d.
bound.

6. Idem Liber, pot 12mo, 1 s. 8d. bound.

7. Grammaticæ Latinæ Inftitutiones, facili, et ad Puerorum
captum accommodata, Methodo Perfcriptæ ; Thoma Ruddi-
manno, A. M. Auctore, editio decima tertia, 12mo, 2 s.
bound.

8. The Rudiments of the Latin Tongue; or, A plain and
eafy Introduction to Latin Grammar: wherein the principles
of the language are medothically digefted both in Englifh and
Latin, with ufeful Notes and Obfervations, explaining the

Y

Terms of Grammar, and farther improving its Rules. By Tho.
Ruddiman, M. A. The twenty-second edition, carefully
corrected and improved, 12mo, 1 s. bound.

9. Grammatical Exercifes ; or, An Exemplification of the
feveral Moods and Tenfes, and of the principal Rules of Con-
ftruction ; confifting chiefly of Moral Sentences, collected out
of the beft Roman Authors, and tranflated into Englifh, to be
rendered back into Latin, the Latin Words being all in the
oppofite Column, taken for the moft part from Mr. Turner's
Exercifes to the Accidence, and adapted to the Method of Mr.
Ruddiman's Latin Rudiments, 18mo, 1 s. bound.

10. Georgii Buchanani Scoti, Poetarum fui feculi facile
Principis, Paraphrafis Pfalmorum Davidis Poetica, ad optimam
editionem Thomæ Ruddimanni, A. M. fummo ftudio recognita
et caftigata. Præmiffa eft accuratior quam antehac carminum'
explicatio, 18mo, 1 s. bound.

11. G. Buchanani Paraphrafis Pfalmorum Davidis Poetica.
Cum verfione Anglica, in qua verbum de verbo, quantum fieri
potuit, redditur : Necnon cum ordine Syntaxeos, in eadem
Pagina. Andrea Waddell, A. M. auctore, editio nova, fumma
cura caftigata, 8vo, 5 s. bound.

12. Titi Livii Hiftoriarum ab Urbe condita libri quinque
priores, ad optimam T. Ruddimanni editionem fideliter ex-
preffi ; ufui fcholarum, 12mo, 2 s. bound.

13. Maturini Corderii Colloquiorum Centuria felecta ; or,
A Select Century of M. Cordery's Colloquies ; with an Englifh tranflation, as literal as poffible, and a large vocabulary
for the affiftance of beginners in the ftudy of Latin, 18mo,
1 s. bound.

14. Maturini Corderii Colloquiorum Centuria felecta, Notis
Anglicis adfperfa, et a plurimis, quæ vulgares editiones
infeftas habent, mendis repurgata, a Gulielmo Willymott,
A. M. Coll. Regal. Cantab. Socio ; ufui fcholarum. Editio
nova, prioribus emendatior, 8d. bound.

15. An Introduction to Latin Syntax; or, An Exemplification of the Rules of Construction, as delivered in Mr. Ruddiman's Rudiments, without anticipating posterior Rules; containing, 1. The Rules of Syntax, with a brief Illustration; 2. Explanatory Notes; 3. Examples taken for the most part from the Claffic Authors; 4. Englifh Exercifes. To which is subjoined, An Epitome of Ancient Hiftory, from the Creation to the Birth of Chrift, intended as a proper mean to initiate Boys in the ufeful Study of Hiftory, while at the fame time it ferves to improve them in the Knowledge of the Latin Tongue. To which is added, a proper Collection of Hiftorical and Chronological Queftions; with a Copious Index. By John Mair, A. M. 12mo, 2 s. bound.

16. Excerpta ex Luciani Operibus, in ufum Juventutis Academicæ, 12mo, 2 s. 6d. half bound.

17. Capita quædam ex Libris M. Fabii Quinctiliani de Inftitutione Oratoria felecta; in ufum Studioforum Claff. Log. et Rhet. 12mo, 2 s. bound.

18. Synopfis of Lectures on Logic and Belles Lettres, read in the Univerfity of Glafgow, Part I. 12mo, 1 s. 9 d. fewed.—The remainder will be publifhed next winter.

19. Manual of French Grammar. To which is added, a fmall Collection from French Authors, in profe and verfe. Intended chiefly for the ufe of fchools. By Lockhart Muirhead, M. A. 12mo, 2 s. bound.

Moft of thofe Claffics and School-books were printed at the Glafgow Univerfity Prefs. A Greek Rudiments, on the plan of Ruddiman's Rudiments of the Latin Tongue, is in preparation by Dr. Doig, Rector of the Grammar School of Stirling.

20. The Works of the Britifh Poets, with Prefaces Biographical and Critical, by Robert Anderfon, M. D. 13 vols. royal 8vo, embellifhed with emblematical vignettes, 8 l. boards.

This Collection includes the Works of One Hundred and Fifteen different Authors, Forty-fix of whom are not in any other edition of the Britifh Poets.

21. Anderfon's Collection of Poetical Tranflations, being the 12th and 13th vols. of the above work, from the Greek and Latin Poets ; containing thofe of Pope, Weft, Dryden, Pitt, Rowe, Hoole, Pye, Cook, Fawkes, Creech, Grainger, &c. 2 vols. royal 8vo, 1 l. 4 s. boards.

22. The Life of Dr. Samuel Johnfon, with Critical Obfervations on his Works, by Robert Anderfon, M. D. 8vo, 5 s. boards.

23. The Mifcellaneous Works of Tobias Smollett, M. D. with Memoirs of his Life and Writings, by Robert Anderfon, M. D. containing, The Adventures of Roderick Random— The Adventures of Peregrine Pickle—Plays and Poems—The Adventures of Ferdinand Count Fathom—The Adventures of Sir Launcelot Greaves—Travels through France and Italy— The Expedition of Humphry Clinker—and, The Adventures of an Atom—6 vols. 8vo, printed on a wove paper, hot-preffed, 2 l. 14 s. bound.

24. The fame book, 6 vols. 12mo, 1 l. 10 s. bound.

25. The Poetical Works of Robert Blair, containing—The Grave—and a Poem to the Memory of Mr. Law—to which is prefixed, the Life of the Author, by Robert Anderfon, M. D. fmall 8vo, 1 s. fewed.

26. A Summary View of Heraldry in reference to the Ufages of Chivalry, and the General Economy of the Feudal Syftem. With an Appendix refpecting fuch Diftinctions of Rank as have place in the Britifh Conftitution, by Thomas Brydfon, F. A. S. royal 8vo, 10 s. 6 d. boards.

27. Agricultural Survey of Argyllfhire, with Plates, and a large Map of the County, by John Smith, D. D. Honorary Member of the Antiquarian and Highland Societies of Scotland, 8vo, 8 s. boards.

28. The fame book in royal 8vo, hot-preffed, 12 s. boards.

29. Archæologia Græca ; or, The Antiquities of Greece, by John Potter, D. D. late Lord Bifhop of Oxford, 2 vols, 8vo, 16 s. bound.

30. The Ancient Hiftory of the Egyptians, Carthaginians, Affyrians, Babylonians, Medes and Perfians, Macedonians and Grecians, by Mr. Rollin, late Principal of the Univerfity of Paris, the ninth edition, 10 vols. 12mo, with plates, 1 l. 15 s. bound.

31. An Effay concerning Human Underftanding, with Thoughts on the Conduct of the Underftanding, by John Locke, Efq. To which is prefixed the Life of the Author, 3 vols. 12mo, 9 s. bound.

32. The Young Miffes Magazine; containing Dialogues between a Governefs and feveral Young Ladies of Quality, her Scholars; in which each Lady is made to fpeak according to her particular Genius, Temper, and Inclination:—Their feveral Faults are pointed out, and the eafy way to mend them, as well as to think, and fpeak, and act properly ; no lefs care being taken to form their Hearts to Goodnefs, than to enlighten their Underftandings with ufeful Knowledge.—A fhort and clear Abridgment is alfo given of Sacred and Profane Hiftory, and fome Leffons in Geography.—The ufeful is blended throughout with the agreeable, the whole being interfperfed with proper Reflections and Moral Tales. Tranflated from the French of Mademoifelle de Beaumont, 2 vols. 18mo, 4 s. bound.

33. A Differtation on Miracles, containing an Examination of the Principles of David Hume, Efq. in an Effay on Miracles, by the late George Campbell, D. D. Principal of the Marifchal College, and one of the Minifters of Aberdeen, the third edition, 12mo, 3 s. 6 d. bound.

34. A Paraphrafe on the Four Evangelifts ; wherein, for the clearer underftanding of the Sacred Hiftory, the whole Text and Paraphrafe are printed in feparate columns overagainft each other ; with Critical Notes on the more difficult Paffages, very ufeful for Families, by Sam. Clarke, D. D. late Rector of St. James's, Weftminfter, 2 vols. 8vo, 12 s. boards.

35. A Paraphrafe on the Acts of the Holy Apoftles, and upon all the Epiftles of the New Teftament, being a complete

Supplement to Dr. Clarke's Paraphrafe on the Four Gofpels ; with Notes, and a fhort Preface to each Epiftle, fhowing the Occafion and Defign of it, with the feveral Arguments fet at the head of each Chapter, and a general Index to all the principal Matters, Words, and Phrafes of the New Teftament, excepting the Revelation. For the ufe of Families. By Thomas Pyle, M. A. Minifter of Lynn-Regis in Norfolk, and Prebendary of the Cathedral Church of Sarum, 2 vols. 8vo, 12 s. boards.

36. A Paraphrafe, with Notes, on the Revelation of St. John, which completes the Paraphrafe on the New Teftameht, in the manner of Dr. Clarke, by Thomas Pyle, M. A. Minifter of Lynn-Regis in Norfolk, and Prebendary of the Cathedral Church of Sarum. The fecond edition, with the laft Manufcript Additions of the Author, now for the firft time incorporated with the work, 8vo, 6s. boards.

The three Publications laft enumerated, form together a complete Commentary on the New Teftament.

37. The Works of Edward Young, LL. D. to which is prefixed the Life of the Author, by Robert Anderfon, M. D. 3 vols. 12mo, 10 s. 6d. bound.

38. Mandeville's Fable of the Bees ; or, Private Vices Public Benefits. With an Effay on Charity and Charity-Schools, and a Search into the Nature of Society : alfo, a Vindication of the Book from the Afperfions contained in a Prefentment of the Grand Jury of Middlefex, and an abufive Letter to Lord C———, 8vo, 8 s. bound.

39. The Poems of Offian, the Son of Fingal, tranflated by James Macpherfon, Efq. 3 vols. 18mo, 6 s. bound.

40. A Catalogue of the Royal and Noble Authors of England, with Lifts of their Works, a new edition, 8vo, 7 s. bound.

41. Eloifa ; or, a Series of Original Letters, collected and publifhed by Mr J. J. Rouffeau, citizen of Geneva. Tranflated from the French. To which are added, the Adventures of Lord B——— at Rome, being the Sequel of Eloifa, found

among the Author's Papers after his Decease, 3 vols. 12mo, 10s. 6d. bound.

The above is translated by Dr. Kenrick, and has been deemed the best translated book in the English language.

42. Illustrations of Hume's Essays, in Answer to Dr. Gregory of Edinburgh, 8vo, 1 s. 6d. stitched.

43. Letters of Junius, 8vo, 7s. bound.

44. Letters of Junius, 12mo, 3s. 6d. bound.

45. Sacontala; or, The Fatal Ring, an Indian Drama, by Calidas. Translated from the original Sanscrit and Pracrit, 12mo, 3 s. 6d. bound.

46. A System of Dissections, explaining the Anatomy of the Human Body, the Manner of displaying the Parts, and their Varieties in Disease, with plates, by Charles Bell. Part First, containing the Dissections of the Abdominal Muscles and Viscera, folio, 5 s. 6d. stitched.

47. The Children's Miscellany; consisting of Select Stories, Fables, and Dialogues, for the Instruction and Amusement of young Persons, 4 parts, 1 s. sewed.

48. The Christian Economy, translated from the original Greek of an old Manuscript found in the Island of Patmos, where St. John wrote his Book of the Revelation, 18mo, 1 s. bound.

49. Visions, translated from the Spanish of Don Francisco de Quevedo. To which is prefixed, an Account of the Life and Writings of the Author, royal 12mo, 5 s. bound.

50. Self-knowledge: A Treatise showing the Nature and Benefit of the important Science, and the Way to attain it. Intermixed with various Reflections and Observations on Human Nature, by John Mason, A. M. 18mo, 2 s. bound.

51. Thoughts in Prison, in five parts, viz. The Imprisonment—the Retrospect—Public Punishment—the Trial—Futurity—by the Rev. William Dodd, LL. D. To which are added, his Last Prayer, written in the night before his death—the Convict's Address to his unhappy Brethren—and other Mis-

ecllaneous Pieces, with some Account of the Author, 18mo, 2 s. bound.

52. Reflections on Death, by William Dodd, LL. D. late Chaplain to the Magdalen, 2 s. 6 d. bound.

53. A Discourse concerning the Nature and Design of the Lord's Supper, in which the principal Things relating to this Institution are briefly considered, and shown to arise out of one single Notion of it, viz. as a Memorial of the Death of Christ. By Henry Grove. To which are added, 1. A Discourse on the Obligations to communicate, and an Answer to the usual Pleas for neglecting it.—2. Devotional Exercises relating to the Lord's Supper, 18mo, 1 s. bound.

54. The Works of Mrs. Elizabeth Rowe, containing Letters from the Dead to the Living—Letters Moral and Entertaining—Devout Exercises of the Heart, in Meditation, in Soliloquy, Prayer, Praise, &c.—Poems and Translations by Mr. Thomas Rowe—Miscellaneous Poems and Translations—Hymns, Odes, and Psalms—Devout Soliloquies—a Paraphrase on Canticles, in blank verse—the History of Joseph, a Poem—Dialogues—Familiar Letters—Life of the Author, &c. &c. &c. 4 vols. small 8vo, 16 s. bound.

55. Letters on the Improvement of the Mind, addressed to a Young Lady, by Mrs. Chapone, 18mo, 2 s. bound.

56. The Economy of Human Life, complete in two parts. Translated from an Indian Manuscript. To which is prefixed, an Account of the Manner in which the said Manuscript was discovered, in a Letter from an English Gentleman residing at China, to the Earl of ***********, 32mo, 1 s. bound.

57. Address to Loch Lomond, a poem, 4to, 1 s. 6 d. stitched.

58. Epistle from Lady Grange to Edward D———, Esq. written during her Confinement in the Island of St. Kilda, 4to, 2 s. stitched.

59. A Paraphrase, or large Explicatory Poem upon the Song of Solomon. Wherein the mutual love of Christ and

his Church, contained in that Old Teftament Song, is imitated
in the Language of the New Teftament, and adapted to the
Gofpel Difpenfation, by the late Rev. Mr. Ralph Erfkine, M.A.
Minifter of the Gofpel at Dunfermline. A new edition, collated
with the folio edition publifhed in 1765, 18mo, 1 s. bound.

60. The Diftilleries Confidered, in their Connection with
the Agriculture, Commerce, and Revenue of Britain ; alfo, in
their Effects upon the Health, Tranquillity, and Morals of the
People, 8vo, 1 s. ftitched.

61. The Impolicy of Partial Taxation demonftrated; particularly as it refpects the Exemption of the Highlands of Scotland from a great part of the Licence Duty chargeable on the
Diftillation of Corn Spirits, 8vo, 1 s. ftitched.

62. Plans for the Defence of Great Britain and Ireland,
by Lieut. Col. Dirom, Deputy Quarter-mafter-general in North
Britain, 8vo, 2 s. 6d. fewed.

Speedily will be publifhed,

1. Lectures on the Nature and End of the Sacred Office,
and on the Dignity, Duty, Qualifications, and Character of the
Sacred Order, by John Smith, D.D. in 1 vol. 8vo.

2. The Life of Tobias Smollet, M.D. with Critical Obfervations on his Works, by Robert Anderfon, M.D. the third
edition, corrected and enlarged.

3. The Method of Teaching and Studying the Belles
Lettres; or, An Introduction to Languages, Poetry, Rhetoric,
Hiftory, Moral Philofophy, Phyfics, &c. With Reflections on
Tafte, and Inftructions with regard to the Eloquence of the
Pulpit, the Bar, and the Stage. The whole illuftrated with
Paffages from the moft famous Poets and Orators ancient and

Z

modern, with Critical Remarks on them. Defigned more particularly for Students in the Univerfities. By Mr. Rollin, late
Principal of the Univerfity of Paris, Profeffor of Eloquence
in the Royal College, and Member of the Royal Academy of
Infcriptions and Belles Lettres. Tranflated from the French,
4 vols, 12mo.

4. The Hiftory, Civil and Commercial, of the Britifh Co-
lonies in the Weft Indies, abridged from the Works of Bryan
Edwards, Efq. with a Map of the Weft India Iflands, 1 vol.
8vo.   : ·

5. The Fifth Edition of Fourcroy's Elements of Chemiftry ;
with numerous Notes, by John Thomfon, Fellow of the Royal
College of Surgeons, and Honorary Member of the Natural
Hiftory Society of Edinburgh, &c. &c. in 3 vols. royal 8vo.